NATURAL RESOURCE MANAGEMENT

NATURAL RESOURCE MANAGEMENT

UNITED STATES GOVERNMENT
ACCOUNTABILITY OFFICE

Nova Science Publishers, Inc
New York

For permission to use material from this book please contact us:
Telephone 631-231-7269; Fax 631-231-8175
Web Site: http://www.novapublishers.com

LIBRARY OF CONGRESS CATALOGING-IN-PUBLICATION DATA

Available Upon Request
ISBN: 978-1-60692-055-8

Published by Nova Science Publishers, Inc. ≃ New York

CONTENTS

ABBREVIATIONS

BLM	Bureau of Land Management
CDOW	Colorado Division of Wildlife
CEQ	Council on Environmental Quality
Challenge	Blackfoot Challenge
Council	Steens Mountain Advisory Council
CMPA	Cooperative Management and Protection Area
Day 2 report	White House Conference report, *Supplemental Analysis of Day Two Facilitated Discussion Sessions*
Forum	Onslow Bight Conservation Forum
GIS	Geographic Information System
Initiative	Cooperative Sagebrush Initiative
Interior	Department of the Interior
MOU	Memorandum of Understanding
NEPA	National Environmental Policy Act
OMB	Office of Management and Budget
Steens Act	Steens Mountain Cooperative Management and Protection Act
USDA	United States Department of Agriculture

Chapter 1

RESULTS IN BRIEF[*]

The experts whose work we reviewed generally consider collaborative resource management as an effective approach for managing natural resources, although they identify a few limitations to its use. According to the experts, collaborative resource management can be effective in reducing and averting conflict and litigation, while at the same time producing better natural resource conditions and strengthening community relationships. The experts noted that successful collaborative efforts use similar practices such as (1) developing open and transparent decision-making processes among the participants, (2) finding leaders of the group, (3) identifying a common goal, and (4) leveraging resources, including funds. Overall, experts considered collaborative efforts successful if they broadened participation and increased cooperation in managing natural resources, or improved natural resource conditions. However, according to many experts, collaboration does have some limitations, such as the fact that building relationships and reaching consensus take time and resources. While many experts see collaboration as an effective approach, a few of the experts question federal agencies' involvement in such efforts, arguing that it can favor local over national interests, allow particular interests to dominate over others, result in a "least common denominator" decision that inadequately protects natural resources, or inappropriately transfer federal authority to local groups.

Of the seven collaborative efforts we studied, most have reduced or averted conflicts in managing natural resource problems and several have achieved site-specific resource results. Specifically, through participants'

---

[*] Excerpted from GAO Report GAO-08-262, dated February 2008.

cooperation, most of these groups were able to avert conflicts that arose—or that might have arisen—from efforts to solve such natural resource problems as threatened and endangered species, lack of wildland fire, invasive species, and degraded wildlife habitat. The efforts that reduced or averted conflicts used many of the collaborative practices identified by the experts, including finding a common goal, using incentives to carry out activities, leveraging available funding, and gathering and using common information. For example, after decades of fire suppression, the Malpai Borderlands Group in southern Arizona and New Mexico successfully reintroduced fire to help regenerate grasses and reduce shrubs in its grassland ecosystem, and dealt with concerns about endangered species surviving such fires. The group worked together to develop a common vision and goal for restoring fire and then sought funding for research to demonstrate that the effects of fire on such species as the lesser long-nose bat and its food source, the agave plant, were not detrimental. Furthermore, several of the collaborative efforts we studied said that they are monitoring different natural resources and are achieving their goals for improving natural resource conditions. However, the extent of the resource improvements and progress toward solving overall landscape-level problems was difficult to assess because some efforts have not yet initiated management activities, while others lack sufficient landscape-level data. For example, the Eastern Upper Peninsula Partners in Ecosystem Management group in Michigan created ecological maps for its planning area but has not monitored any changes in ecological conditions at a landscape level since it has been working together. The participants said that, because the group's primary purpose is to share information to help participants plan their own work, the group does not need to conduct landscape-level monitoring.

Federal land and resource management agencies face several challenges in participating in collaborative resource management efforts, according to the experts, federal officials, and participants in collaborative efforts whom we interviewed. Key challenges that the agencies face fall within the following major areas:

- Improving employees' collaborative skills. Often, federal employees are technical experts and may not have the skills and experience to collaborate. Collaborative skills include the ability to conduct meetings, involve relevant stakeholders, resolve disputes, and share technical information to make it accessible to groups. Federal participants in collaborative groups we studied said that federal staff need to have such skills, in addition to their technical skills, to work effectively with such groups. Improving federal employees' collaborative skills can enable them to work more effectively with a collaborative group.

- Determining whether to participate in a particular collaborative effort. Collaborative resource management efforts often begin with local communities, and federal agencies can determine what role they can have in the effort. External factors, such as a community's collaborative capacity and the amount of controversy involved, often affect whether a group may succeed. Federal participants we interviewed said that opportunities to collaborate continually emerge as community members initiate efforts. However, without understanding the external factors that may affect success, federal land and resource management agencies may become involved and invest resources in a collaborative effort that has little chance of succeeding.
- Sustaining federal employees' participation over time. According to some groups and federal participants we interviewed, federal participation in collaborative efforts is critical to getting work accomplished. In particular, the agency employees can contribute scientific and technical expertise, such as habitat identification and mapping skills, to help plan and focus the group's work. However, federal land and resource management agency field offices that we visited have downsized in the last several years, leaving fewer staff available for collaborative efforts. Federal participants in collaborative efforts we interviewed stated that with fewer staff, less time and effort can be spent on collaboration. Limited participation by federal agencies may constrain the amount of work that can be planned and therefore accomplished by both the agency and the group.
- Measuring participation and monitoring results to ensure accountability. Participation in and natural resource results of collaborative efforts are difficult to measure and collaborative efforts often lack a systematic approach for monitoring the results. Federal participants we interviewed noted that there are no effective methods available to measure and account for participation in collaborative efforts, making it difficult for them to show the results of the time and resources expended working with collaborative groups. A lack of measuring or monitoring data may make it difficult for agencies and their partners to demonstrate and be accountable for their results and justify their continued participation.
- Sharing agency and group experiences with collaboration. Collaborative groups are unique in their makeup, organization, circumstances, and abilities, but can face similar problems working together and with federal agencies. Groups are scattered throughout

the United States, and do not have many opportunities to meet and share experiences. Although Web sites and guidebooks exist to share information, without venues to bring collaborative groups together, it is more difficult for group members to learn and benefit directly from each other's experience.

- Working within the framework of federal statutes and agency policies to support collaboration. Experts and collaborative groups have identified some federal laws and agency policies as being inconsistent with collaboration. For example, USDA and Interior have implemented federal ethics rules differently in determining whether their staff could be members of the nonprofit board managing the Blackfoot Challenge group in Montana, causing some confusion and concerns among the partners. Others identified federal advisory committee rules, the National Environmental Policy Act, and the Endangered Species Act as being inconsistent with collaboration. These authorities and policies reflect processes established to support good government practices, such as transparency and accountability. Without evaluating the laws and policies involved, the federal agencies cannot determine the changes needed to better balance collaboration with good government practices.

Through the federal interagency task force charged with pursuing proposed actions raised by participants at the 2005 White House Conference on Cooperative Conservation, the federal government has developed policies and taken actions that have made progress in addressing several of these challenges. For example, to enhance federal employees' collaborative skills, the agencies recently identified personnel competencies that encourage collaborative behavior and experience-based training that includes collaboration. In addition, to address difficult and time-consuming aspects of the federal law that directs how federal agencies work with advisory groups—the Federal Advisory Committee Act—agencies are considering ways to simplify the implementation of its requirements. While the policies and actions implemented so far help address several of the challenges that agencies face, the task force has yet to develop and disseminate guidance, tools, and examples that will further address the challenges, such as sharing agency and group experiences with collaboration. Furthermore, the CEQ officials responsible for the Cooperative Conservation initiative recognized that it is a long-term effort that will require the coordinated actions of several interagency teams, departments, and agencies to achieve the vision of cooperative conservation. Yet, the task force is a temporary, voluntary group that has not developed a plan to lay out long-term goals for cooperative conservation and determine how the actions taken to date and in the future will help reach these goals and support collaborative resource management as an approach for managing federal natural resources.

We are making recommendations to the Chairman of CEQ and the Secretaries of Agriculture and the Interior to take several actions that can enhance federal agencies' participation in and support of ongoing and future collaborative efforts, as well as help structure and direct the interagency effort for the long term. The actions that we are recommending include, among others, disseminating tools for assessing collaborative opportunities; developing criteria for others to use in monitoring collaborative efforts particularly at the landscape level; and developing a long-term plan for carrying out cooperative conservation activities including collaborative resource management. In commenting on a draft of this report, Interior and USDA concurred with our conclusions and five of six recommendations. The departments neither agreed nor disagreed with our recommendation that they should develop a joint policy to consistently implement ethics rules governing employee participation in nonprofit boards. USDA's Office of General Counsel noted that while such a policy might be desirable, it may not be feasible. CEQ did not provide comments on the draft report.

Chapter 2

BACKGROUND

Federal efforts to use collaboration, broadly, and collaborative resource management more specifically have their roots in natural resource and environmental law, litigation, and alternative efforts to resolve environmental conflicts. Beginning in the 1960s and 1970s as environmental concerns over species, wilderness preservation, and air and water pollution heightened and legislation to protect different resources followed, litigation over land and resource use became more common. In the 1980s and 1990s, a number of factors, including court decisions and regulatory and economic changes, resulted in decreased timber harvests and increased scrutiny of grazing on public lands. In the 1990s, concerns over pollution and resource problems that cross property lines—such as water quality or endangered species—increased, and sometimes resulted in litigation. Also during this time, development of private lands posed increased threats to habitat, water quality, rural lifestyles, and wildlife, including threatened and endangered species.

Over the same time frame beginning in the 1970s, environmental conflict resolution began to evolve as an alternative way of dealing with environmental disputes outside of the courts. This approach uses facilitation, mediation, and other methods to negotiate solutions among disputing parties. It also involves collaborative efforts to solve problems and conflicts before they have a chance to fully develop. In the 1990s, as these alternatives to litigation became more established, two laws were enacted authorizing their use by federal agencies and the U.S. District Courts—the Administrative Dispute Resolution Act of 1996 and the Alternative Dispute Resolution Act of 1998. Also in 1998, legislation created the U.S. Institute for Environmental Conflict Resolution, a federal institute to assess, and assist in resolving, conflicts related to federal land, natural resource, or environmental management.

Throughout the 1990s, some communities facing natural resource problems decided to use alternative approaches to solving associated conflicts, forming grassroots groups of diverse stakeholders to discuss the problems and develop solutions. The collaborative groups that formed often included federal land and resource management agency representatives as participants. Recognizing the value of these groups, the federal land and resource management agencies began developing programs in support of such efforts. The agencies have been working collaboratively with communities for a long while, but placed increased emphasis on collaboration in the 1990s. Specifically, in 1997, the Forest Service began a partnership program to gather guidance and information on how best to work with local communities. In 2003, Interior began an effort to focus on working cooperatively with local communities on conservation activities, both on public and private lands. In addition, the U.S. Fish and Wildlife Service has a program, called Partners for Fish and Wildlife, to work with private landowners to provide technical and financial assistance in protecting threatened and endangered species on their lands.

More recently, the federal land and natural resource agencies have been authorized by specific legislation to collaborate with nonfederal parties on specific resource problems. For example, both BLM and the Forest Service received authority to use stewardship contracts—which allow them, for example, to use the value of products sold, such as timber, to offset the cost of contracted services such as removing small trees and brush from the forest—to achieve national forest land management goals that meet local and rural community needs.[1]

In 2004, the President signed Executive Order 13352 introducing the Cooperative Conservation initiative to increase the use of collaboration and other processes for managing land, natural resource, and environmental issues. The order directed the Secretaries of Agriculture, Commerce, Defense, and the Interior, and the Administrator of the Environmental Protection Agency to carry out natural resource and environmental laws in a manner that facilitates "cooperative conservation." The order defined this as "actions that relate to the use, enhancement, and enjoyment of natural resources, protection of the environment, or both, and involve collaborative activity among Federal, State, local, and tribal governments, private for-profit and nonprofit institutions, other nongovernmental entities and individuals." The Executive Order is being carried out by CEQ, in its role coordinating federal environmental efforts and working with agencies in the development of environmental policies and initiatives. Also involved is OMB, in its role overseeing the preparation of the federal budget and supervising executive branch agencies. OMB evaluates the effectiveness of agency programs, policies, and procedures, as well as ensuring that agency reports, rules, testimony, and proposed legislation are consistent with the President's budget and with administration policies. In addition, OMB oversees and coordinates the administration's procurement, financial management, information, and regulatory policies.

While collaboration refers broadly to the way different groups work together to achieve a common goal, collaborative resource management efforts involve multiple parties joining together voluntarily to identify environmental and natural resource problems and goals and to design activities and projects to resolve the problems and achieve their goals. The federal agencies work with collaborative resource management groups using partnership tools, which are cooperative or voluntary agreements among the federal and nonfederal groups to share resources and achieve the objectives of all parties.[2] Each of the four major federal land and resource management agencies—BLM, U.S. Fish and Wildlife Service, National Park Service within Interior and USDA's Forest Service—has a complex mix of legislative authorities that allow it to create and fund partnerships. In the simplest form, a partnership can exist without any exchange of funds or items of value from the federal agency to a nonfederal group and a memorandum of agreement or understanding is used to describe the details of the arrangements. In cases when federal funds or property are provided to nonfederal entities as part of a partnership, the agencies use different instruments such as grants or cooperative agreements to document the agreement and work to be done.[3]

Collaborative resource management efforts can involve any mix of the nation's 2.3 billion acres of federal, state, local, private, or tribal land. Historical settlement and development of the nation resulted in the intermingling of lands among these different entities. As shown in figure 1, about 60 percent of the nation's land, or almost 1.4 billion acres, is privately owned and managed, while more than 27 percent, or about 628 million acres, is managed by the four federal land and resource management agencies. More than 43 million acres, representing almost 2 percent of the nation's land, are owned and managed by the federal government for purposes such as military installations and water infrastructure. About 8 percent of the nation's land, or 195 million acres, is owned and managed by state and local governments and more than 2 percent, or about 56 million acres, is held in trust by the federal government for Native American tribes.

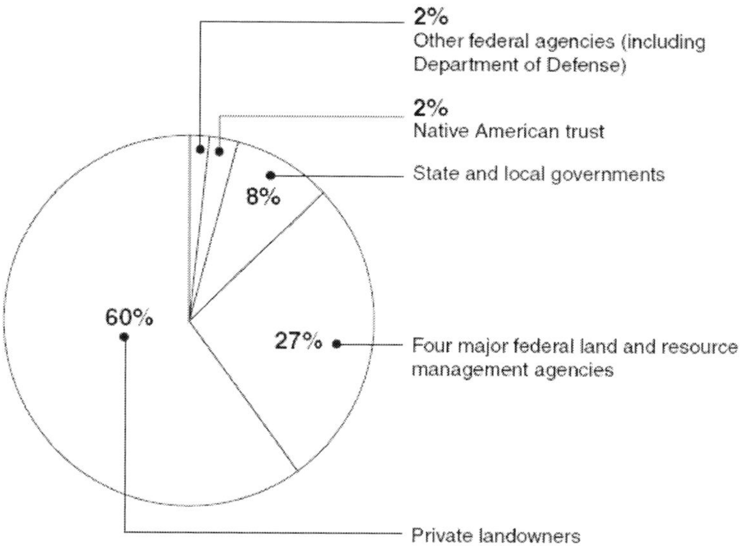

Source: GAO analysis of Congressional Research Service and USDA data.
Note: Percentages do not add due to rounding.

Figure 1. Land Ownership and Management in the United States.

Collaborative efforts are governed by a framework of federal, state, and local laws, as well as federal Indian law and tribal law, that determine how management activities, including collaborative management activities, are carried out. These efforts often involve coordinated decision making for management activities that the collaborative groups undertake. Each land and resource manager or landowner, including federal agencies, retains decision-making authority for the activities that occur on their respective lands and follow applicable requirements to implement them, although the federal agencies may work with other group members to develop and consider plans and gather information and community input. When collaborative activities occur on private lands, individual landowners make decisions about the activities that occur subject to applicable federal, state, and local laws, and decide whether and how to share information related to their lands with members of the group.

LAWS GOVERNING COLLABORATIVE EFFORTS ON FEDERAL LANDS

Collaborative management activities on federal lands are governed by federal resource and environmental laws. Overall, the four federal land management agencies manage their lands for a variety of purposes, although each agency has unique authorities that give it particular responsibilities. Specifically, both BLM and the Forest Service manage lands under their control for multiple uses and to provide a sustained yield of renewable resources such as timber, fish and wildlife, forage for livestock, and recreation. On the other hand, the National Park Service's mission is to conserve the scenery, natural and historic objects, and wildlife of the national park system so that they will remain unimpaired for the enjoyment of current and future generations. The U.S. Fish and Wildlife Service, under its authorities, manages refuges for the conservation, management—and where appropriate—restoration of fish, wildlife, and plant resources and their habitats within the United States, for the benefit of present and future generations.

Other federal agencies—including the military services in the Department of Defense and the power marketing administrations in the Department of Energy—have land and resource management responsibilities that may cause them to become involved in collaborative efforts. The military services—the Army, Navy, Marine Corps, and Air Force—use their lands primarily to train military forces and test weapon systems, but are required under the Sikes Act of 1960 to provide for the conservation and rehabilitation of natural resources on military lands. The power marketing administrations—which include the Western Area Power Administration, Bonneville Power Administration, Southwestern Power Administration, and Southeastern Power Administration—sell and deliver power within the United States on hundreds of miles of transmission lines across public and private land using rights-of-way. Under the Energy Policy Act of 2005, transmission owners, including the power administrations, must maintain the reliability of their transmission systems, which includes establishing and maintaining the vegetation on these rights-of-way so that power lines are not compromised. Lines may be at risk from trees falling on them, electrical arcing from a power line to a tree or other objects in the right-of-way, or forest fires. Other agencies, such as the Department of Transportation and state transportation agencies, conduct activities that affect land and resources, and collaborate with agencies such as the U.S. Fish and Wildlife Service to manage the effects on wildlife and habitat.

Management activities that occur on federal lands, including those developed by a collaborative group are subject to the National Environmental Policy Act (NEPA) of 1969, and the Endangered Species Act of 1973. NEPA requires that federal agencies evaluate the likely environmental effects of proposed projects and plans using an environmental assessment or, if the action would be likely to significantly affect the environment, a more detailed environmental impact statement. The scope of actions being analyzed under NEPA may encompass a broad area, such as an entire national forest, or a specific project such as treatment of invasive species on several acres of land. The federal agencies are mandated to include the public in the NEPA process through efforts such as providing public notice of meetings, making related environmental documents available to the public, and considering public comments. Under the Endangered Species Act, federal agencies are required to consult with the U.S. Fish and Wildlife Service to ensure that any activities they carry out do not jeopardize the continued existence of a threatened or endangered species or destroy or harm any habitat that is critical for the conservation of the species.[4]

Laws Governing Collaborative Efforts on State, Local, Private, and Tribal Lands

Collaborative activities that occur on state, local, and private lands are subject to state and local laws that provide authority for numerous agencies to manage state and local lands and programs to protect and conserve natural resources, as well as generate revenue from these resources. Many states have trust lands that were granted to them at statehood by the federal government. These lands, which constitute 46 million acres of the continental United States, are typically managed to produce revenue for beneficiaries such as schools and other public institutions. As a result, the primary uses of these state lands are activities that may generate revenue such as livestock grazing, oil and gas leasing, hard rock mining, and timber. In addition, states regulate land and natural resource use through a variety of programs, such as wildlife management or forestry programs. Each state manages fish and wildlife through various programs, and these state wildlife programs typically manage certain species of wildlife as game for recreation purposes. These programs may also own and manage land with habitat particularly suited for game species, and sometimes provide protection for particular species of concern. State forestry agencies, which are also in every state, can manage their state forests for uses such as timber or recreation.

Private landowners determine how, or whether, to implement collaborative activities on their lands, consistent with applicable federal, state, and local laws and zoning restrictions that regulate the types of activities that can occur on particular areas of land including open space, agricultural, residential, commercial, and industrial lands. For example, a nonprofit organization, such as The Nature Conservancy, can own land solely for conservation purposes, while a timber company uses its lands to harvest timber for profit. Private activities must also be consistent with applicable federal environmental laws such as the Endangered Species Act. Under the act, private landowners are not required to consult with the U.S. Fish and Wildlife Service on activities they conduct on their land, but the act prohibits them from "taking" a threatened or endangered species.[5] In certain cases, private landowners may obtain permits for taking species if the taking is incidental to a lawful activity. To obtain such a permit, a landowner must submit a habitat conservation plan to the U.S. Fish and Wildlife Service that specifies the likely effect of the landowner's activities on a listed species and mitigation measures that the landowner will implement. Landowners may also enter into voluntary safe harbor agreements with the U.S. Fish and Wildlife Service in which landowners manage habitat for endangered species in return for assurances that no additional restrictions will be imposed as a result of their conservation actions.

Land use activities, such as harvesting trees for timber, applying fertilizer and pesticides for agriculture, and diverting water for irrigation or other use, can degrade air and water quality and habitat for wildlife. However, undeveloped lands used for forestry, livestock grazing, and agriculture—in addition to producing the nation's food and fiber—are vital to the protection of the nation's environment and natural resources. To encourage conservation on private lands used for agricultural and natural resource production, USDA operates approximately 20 voluntary conservation programs that are designed to address a range of environmental concerns—soil erosion, surface and ground water quantity and quality, air quality, loss of wildlife habitat and native species, and others—by compensating landowners for taking certain lands out of production or using certain conservation practices on lands in production.[6] Among these programs, USDA's Natural Resources Conservation Service manages the Environmental Quality Incentives Program, which promotes agricultural production and environmental quality as compatible national goals and provides technical and financial assistance to farmers and ranchers to address soil, water, air, and related natural resource concerns and to comply with environmental laws, and the Wetlands Reserve Program, which authorizes technical and financial assistance to eligible landowners to restore, enhance, and protect wetlands. Since its beginning as the Soil Conservation Service more than 70 years ago, the service has delivered its assistance to farmers and ranchers through partnerships with locally led conservation districts.

Resource and land use decisions on Indian lands are governed by federal Indian law and tribal law. Federal Indian law includes relevant provisions of the Constitution, treaties with Indian tribes, federal statutes and regulations, executive orders, and judicial opinions that collectively regulate the relationships among Indian nations, the United States, and individual state governments. Tribal law includes the constitutions, statutes, regulations, judicial opinions, and tradition and customs of individual tribes.

Chapter 3

EXPERTS GENERALLY VIEW COLLABORATIVE RESOURCE MANAGEMENT AS AN EFFECTIVE APPROACH FOR IMPROVING THE MANAGEMENT OF NATURAL RESOURCES, BUT A FEW QUESTION COLLABORATION INVOLVING FEDERALLY MANAGED LANDS

Experts whose literature we reviewed consider collaborative resource management to be effective in managing natural resources because it can reduce or avert conflict and litigation, while at the same time improving natural resource conditions and strengthening community relationships. The experts note that successful groups that are able to achieve these benefits use various collaborative practices. In addition, many experts cite limitations to collaboration and others question collaborative resource management efforts involving federally managed land, arguing that collaborative efforts can favor local interests over national interests, be dominated by particular interests over others, result in a "least common denominator" decision that inadequately protects natural resources, or inappropriately transfer federal authority to local groups.

EXPERTS VIEW COLLABORATION AS AN EFFECTIVE APPROACH FOR IMPROVING NATURAL RESOURCE MANAGEMENT

Experts view collaborative resource management as an effective approach for addressing natural resource problems compared with more traditional approaches, such as independent and uncoordinated decision making or litigation. They note, based on their research of many collaborative efforts, that collaborative resource management offers several benefits, including (1) reduced conflict and litigation; (2) better natural resource results;. (3) shared ownership and authority; (4) increased trust, communication, and understanding among members of a group; and (5) increased community capacity, such as fostering the ability for community members to engage in respectful dialogue. In addition, experts say that effective collaboration can have different structures and processes, but use similar practices.

According to the experts, collaboration can reduce conflict and litigation because it provides a way for people to become directly involved in resolving issues through face-to-face discussions and move beyond the impasse associated with more adversarial approaches. Experts say that the lawsuits, administrative appeals, and lobbying campaigns that have been associated with natural resource management in the past can be expensive and divisive and lead to delays in getting land management activities and projects accomplished. Such was the case in the Applegate watershed in northern California and southwestern Oregon in the early 1990s when years of adversarial conflict between environmentalists, the timber industry, and government agencies over forest management issues and litigation related to these issues had resulted in policy gridlock, with neither side able to effectively achieve its goals. In this case and in many others cited by the experts, stakeholders were driven to try collaboration because they were frustrated with a lack of progress through other means. Through face-to-face discussions, parties may be able to define solutions that meet their mutual interests and avert potentially costly litigation that requires winners and losers and, in some cases, results in delays. For example, according to one of the participants of the Blackfoot Challenge, one of the collaborative efforts we studied, the group was able to prevent litigation by an environmental group over water flows in the Blackfoot River in Montana by implementing conservation programs during drought that increased water levels in the river for fish.

Blackfoot Challenge

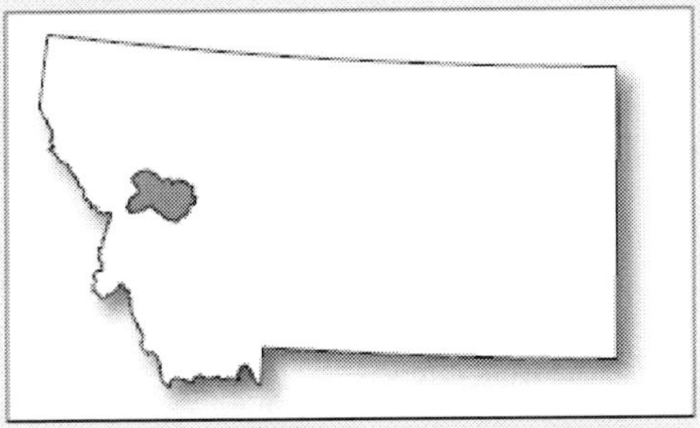

Sources: GAO presentation of Blackfoot Challenge data.

The Blackfoot Challenge collaborative effort was built around the 1.5 million acre Blackfoot River watershed in west-central Montana. The group, which formally joined together in 1993, is working to preserve wildlife habitat and maintain a rural way of life.

This watershed has intermingled lands, 57 percent of which are public lands, 27 percent are private lands, and 16 percent are owned by a timber company. To carry out their efforts, the members formed a nonprofit group that includes federal agencies, state and local agencies, and private landowners.

The experts noted that, in addition to reducing conflict, collaboration can lead to better natural resource results than traditional approaches. A collaborative process, with a range of stakeholders—from local citizens to agency technical specialists, and from environmentalists to industry representatives—incorporates a broad array of knowledge, which may include specialized local knowledge or technical expertise that would not be available to particular stakeholders or agencies if they were working alone. With input from a wide variety of stakeholders, collaborative efforts are often able to identify creative solutions to natural resource problems and make better, more-informed decisions about natural resource management. Because these decisions are made collaboratively and have concurrence from multiple affected stakeholders, solutions are frequently easier to implement with less opposition. A second collaborative effort we studied, the Cooperative Sagebrush Initiative, started in 2006 to involve multiple stakeholders in developing and implementing solutions to conserve sagebrush habitat.

Another benefit noted by experts is that collaborative resource management creates shared ownership of natural resource problems among the stakeholders. The experts recognize that many of the nation's natural resource problems that cross ownership boundaries are not amenable to traditional centralized government solutions through regulation and cannot be solved by single organizations. For example, problems such as the spread of invasive species, the decline of threatened and endangered species, the loss of open space from development and urban sprawl across agricultural landscapes, and non-point-source water pollution—pollution from diffuse sources—are just a few of the numerous challenges resulting from the independent actions of countless individuals. Collaborative efforts bring many of these individuals together, making progress toward resolving the problems possible. In addition, through collaboration, federal and state programs can be made locally relevant and decision making and progress are able to transcend political boundaries. Consequently, local stakeholders feel consulted and may view federal agencies as partners, and programs encourage joint stewardship of public lands.

Experts also noted that collaborative resource management can increase communication, trust, and understanding among different stakeholders. The collaborative process can bring together stakeholders with divergent interests who may have no prior direct experience working together or have an adversarial relationship. As they work together to address a particular common natural resource problem, these stakeholders often begin to develop trust and increase communication. Furthermore, through such communication, stakeholders can become more informed about each other and the natural resource problem and develop an enhanced understanding of its complexities. For example, environmental and industry groups with divergent opinions about natural resource use may be represented in a particular collaborative effort. Through working together in collaborative groups and opening lines of communication, these stakeholders may learn to appreciate each other's perspective by focusing on interests that they have in common. Experts have noted examples in which environmentalists learned to appreciate ranchers' needs to earn a living through grazing livestock, timber companies acknowledge the value of healthy ecosystems, and federal agency technical experts recognized the importance of using traditional knowledge in land management practices. One of the collaborative efforts we studied, the Eastern Upper Peninsula Partners in Ecosystem Management, has shared information to improve forested habitat, including on private timber lands.

Cooperative Sagebrush Initiative

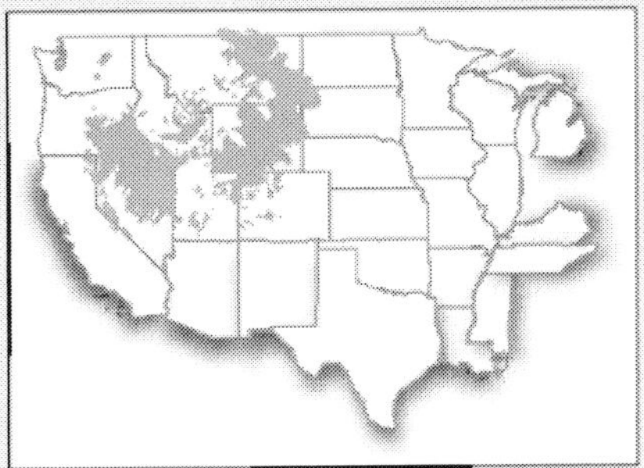

Sources: GAO analysis of U.S. Geological Survey data.

The Cooperative Sagebrush Initiative is a collaborative group that began in 2006 to focus on enhancing the sagebrush range, which spans 11 western states. The Cooperative Sagebrush Initiative incorporated into a nonprofit organization in 2007.

Participants in the effort include representatives from federal agencies such as BLM, U.S. Fish and Wildlife Service, U.S. Geological Survey, and Natural Resources Conservation Service; nonprofit groups such as the Sand County Foundation and the North American Grouse Partnership; energy companies such as Encana Oil and Gas, Peabody Energy, and Shell Oil; and private landowners.

In addition to improving relationships within a collaborative group, experts identify collaboration more broadly as a means to increase the social capacity of a community. Increased community capacity can include developing networks between the public and private sectors and enhancing the public's engagement in issues affecting the community. The experts note that through increasing community capacity, collaborative groups may enable the community to deal better with future problems that arise.

Collaborative groups that are able to achieve these benefits can be organized differently and have different decision making and organizational processes, but use similar practices that distinguish them from more traditional groups and make their efforts more effective and potentially more successful. A collaborative group can be organized formally—such as a legislatively mandated advisory group or an incorporated nonprofit organization—or less formally, with loosely organized members and simple written agreements. Collaborative groups may also employ a variety of processes to manage their meetings and organizations and may strive to achieve different desired outcomes, such as sharing information on what each member is doing, partnering on particular management activities, or seeking agreement on how to manage natural resource problems.

Eastern Upper Peninsula Partners in Ecosystem Management

Source: GAO analysis.

The Eastern Upper Peninsula Partners in Ecosystem Management collaborative group formed in 1992 with the idea of managing neighboring lands in Michigan's eastern Upper Peninsula in a complementary way by sharing information.

The eastern Upper Peninsula includes forests that have historically been managed for timber. The group focuses on about 4 million acres that span the Hiawatha National Forest, the Seney National Wildlife Refuge, Pictured Rocks National Lakeshore, state land, and privately-owned land. The partners include the Forest Service, U.S. Fish and Wildlife Service, National Park Service, Michigan Department of Natural Resources, The Nature Conservancy, and companies owning private forest land.

While group structure and process may differ, many experts identified collaborative practices that groups share and that can contribute to effective collaboration.[7] The experts primarily identified the following practices through studying various existing collaborative resource management efforts:

- Seek inclusive representation. Most of the experts who wrote about collaborative practices noted that all stakeholders—individuals and organizations whose interests are affected by the process or its outcome—should be included in the process by participating or being represented. One expert suggested that such stakeholders may include those affected by any sort of agreement that could be reached, those needed to successfully implement an agreement, and those who could undermine an agreement if not included in the process. Some experts added that participation should be voluntary.
- Develop a collaborative process. Many experts noted that a collaborative process should be designed by the participants to fit the needs and circumstances of their situation. Some experts recommended that groups employ the assistance of a neutral facilitator with experience in building collaborative processes. According to some experts, the process should include decision and process rules to govern how the group operates. For example, collaborative groups may use consensus to make decisions, described by several experts as a process in which discussion proceeds until all viewpoints are heard and the stakeholders, or most of the stakeholders, are willing to agree to a conclusion or course of action. When using consensus, some experts note that a group should agree on what consensus means and what the responsibilities are for parties who disagree, such as providing an alternative. In addition to establishing decision rules, one expert noted that participants need to identify the roles and responsibilities for implementing an agreement and obtain commitment from the participants that an agreement will be implemented.
- Pursue flexibility, openness, and respect. According to many experts, flexibility, transparency, and respect should be built into the collaborative process. Flexibility is important in the process in order to accommodate changing timetables, issues, data needs, interests, and knowledge. Transparency and open communication are essential for maintaining trust and can be achieved through maintaining a written record of proceedings and decisions and ensuring that all parties have equal access to relevant information. Having a respectful process is also necessary to attain civil discourse in which participants listen to one another, take each participant's perspectives seriously, and attempt to address the concerns of each participant. Building respect and openness involves accepting the diverse values, interests, and knowledge—including local knowledge—of the parties involved.
- Find leadership. Several experts identified the need for collaborative groups to find a credible leader who is capable of articulating a strong vision. According to the experts, a leader

should have good communication skills, be able to work on all sides of an issue, and ensure that the collaborative process established by the group is followed. Experts noted that neutral facilitators can also function as leaders for a group. In addition, experts said that it is important to build leadership skills within the organizations participating in a group so that these leaders can effectively represent the interests of their organizations.

- Identify or develop a common goal. Most of the experts who wrote about collaborative practices noted the importance of groups having clear goals. In a collaborative process, the participants may not have the same overall interests—in fact they may have conflicting interests. However, by establishing a goal based on what the group shares in common—a sense of place or community, mutual goals, or mutual fears—rather than on where there is disagreement among missions or philosophies, a collaborative group can shape its own vision and define its own purpose. When articulated and understood by the members of a group, this shared purpose provides people with a reason to participate in the process.
- Develop a process for obtaining information. Some experts noted that effective collaborative processes incorporate high-quality information, including both scientific information and local knowledge, accessible to and understandable by all participants. As one expert noted, conflict over issues of fact is capable of incapacitating a collaborative process. Therefore, it is important to develop a common factual base, which can be accomplished by all participants jointly gathering and developing a common understanding of relevant data. This process allows the stakeholders to accept the facts themselves, rather than having the facts disseminated to them through experts.
- Leverage available resources. Many of the experts emphasized that collaboration can take time and resources in order to accomplish such activities as building trust among the participants, setting up the ground rules for the process, attending meetings, conducting project work, and monitoring and evaluating the results of work performed. Consequently, it is important for groups to ensure that they identify and leverage sufficient funding to get the group started and to accomplish the objectives. One expert noted that many collaborative groups are successful in attracting sufficient funding for restoration projects but have difficulty in securing funding for administration of the group.
- Provide incentives. Some experts note that economic incentives can help collaborative efforts achieve their goals. For example, by purchasing conservation easements, a group can give landowners incentives to help achieve the goal of preserving open space. A

conservation easement is a restriction placed on a parcel of land that limits certain types of uses or prevents development from taking place in order to protect the resources associated with the land. By purchasing easements and thus creating an incentive for a landowner to keep the land in its current land use, the groups are able to keep the land from being developed, preserving open space and providing other ecological benefits.

- Monitor results for accountability. According to many experts, to be effective, the participants in groups need to be accountable to their constituencies and to the process that they have established. In addition, organizations supporting the process expect accountability for the time, effort, money, or patience they invested in the group. As a result, experts note the importance of designing protocols to monitor and evaluate progress toward a collaborative group's goals, from both an environmental and a social perspective. Some experts recommend that collaborative groups use monitoring as a part of an adaptive management approach that involves modifying management strategies or project implementation based on the results of initial activities.

While experts noted that these practices are commonly shared by successful collaborative groups, one expert said that the use of the collaborative practices does not guarantee a group's success. To measure whether groups are successful, experts noted that two criteria can be used: (1) whether the groups were able to increase participation and cooperation and (2) whether they improved natural resource conditions. The first criterion measures success based on organizational factors and social outcomes, such as improved relations and trust among stakeholders. In many instances, the groups studied by one expert identified factors such as improved communication and understanding as their greatest success. Factors used by some experts to evaluate success in this respect include the perceived effects of the collaborative effort in building relationships, the extent of agreement reached, and educating and outreaching to members of the community. The second criterion for success is based on whether groups have been able to improve natural resource conditions as measured by specific indicators, such as water quality, ecosystem health, or species recovery. Some experts note that to evaluate progress toward improving resource conditions, monitoring needs to be performed over a period long enough for change to occur and focus on indicators that are associated with a group's natural resource goals.

Many Experts Identified Limitations of Collaboration and a Few Raise Questions about Using It on Federally Managed Lands

Although collaborative resource management is generally viewed by the experts as an effective approach for addressing natural resource problems, many experts discussed two limitations to its use. First, the process of collaboration, which involves bringing people together to work on a problem and moving the group forward to reach a decision, can be difficult and time-consuming, particularly in the initial stages when the group is getting started, and thus require large amounts of resources, including staff and money. Even after a group has been working together for a period of time, there may be inefficiencies with the process as new group members need to be brought up to speed.

Second, collaboration does not always work in providing the solution to all natural resource problems. In some instances, for example when there are irreconcilable differences among group members, agreement may not be possible. In other instances, one particular stakeholder may derail the process by refusing to cooperate. As a result, collaborative resource management is not applicable everywhere, and collaborative efforts may not be replicable. For example, collaboration may not work in a community deeply divided over a particular natural resource issue that has generated a long history of controversy and litigation even though a collaborative effort dealing with the same issue was successful in another community.

Furthermore, some experts question whether collaborative resource management groups are equitable; have balanced power; produce solutions that are protective of the environment; and are accountable to the public, particularly in circumstances where federally managed lands are involved. A number of experts raised concern over the equity of collaboration, noting that it can remove discussions from the public arena and empower those who are involved in the group at the expense of those who cannot, or choose not to, participate even though they have a legitimate interest. By their nature, collaborative groups tend to be primarily made up of local stakeholders. Yet, others who may not live in the community but have an interest in the lands because they recreate there, use water originating there, or value endangered species living there are sometimes left out of the process because they are unaware it is occurring or do not have the means or the resources to participate. For example, national environmental organizations cannot always participate in local efforts because they may not have people at these locations or be able to bear the expense of traveling there.

Some experts also question collaboration on the grounds that public processes may be co-opted by parties with particular interests who manage to control the agenda of the group. Many experts raising this question were concerned about local economic interests taking over a process and, because of their influence, overriding other interests. Yet, one expert noted concerns that the process could also be co-opted by environmental interests. Furthermore, some experts critical of collaborative resource management raised concerns about the efforts focusing on reaching a consensus decision. By trying to reach consensus, they argued, compromises are made that can result in a "least common denominator" solution, which some may view as less protective of the natural resources.

Finally, a few experts criticize collaborative efforts designed to make decisions about management activities on federal lands because they believe collaboration reduces federal agencies' accountability to the broader public. Specifically, some of these experts say that collaboration effectively transfers the authority to make land management decisions from the federal land management agencies to local citizens. Consequently, these experts argue that when collaborative groups make decisions related to federal land, the land and resource management agencies do not carry out their legal responsibilities to manage the public land and are not accountable to the public.

In response to such questions raised about collaboration, other experts note that a well-designed and implemented collaborative process can avoid some of the outcomes with which the critics of collaboration are concerned. For example, a process that is inclusive will incorporate both local and national interests, and a process that uses the leadership of a neutral facilitator can help to ensure that all viewpoints are considered and prevent any one group from taking over the process. Furthermore, one expert notes that a well-designed collaborative process that includes debate over the facts of an issue can avoid a "least common denominator" solution. Finally, according to an expert, when participating in collaborative groups that are transparent, federal agencies can show that they are not improperly transferring authority to local communities.

Chapter 4

Most Collaborative Efforts We Studied Reduced or Averted Resource Conflicts, Completed Projects, and Improved Natural Resource Conditions to an Extent That Could Not Be Determined

Overall, the collaborative resource management efforts that we studied were successful in achieving participation and cooperation among their members and sustaining or improving natural resource conditions, the two criteria the experts identified to gauge the success of collaborative groups. Six of the seven collaborative efforts we studied have reduced or averted the kinds of conflicts that often arise when dealing with contentious natural resource problems, particularly those that cross property boundaries, such as threatened and endangered species, lack of wildland fire, invasive species, degraded wildlife habitat, or similar problems. However, the extent of resource improvement across broader landscapes that the efforts were working in was difficult to determine because the landscape-level data needed to make such determinations were not always gathered.

MOST COLLABORATIVE RESOURCE MANAGEMENT EFFORTS REDUCED OR AVERTED CONFLICTS THROUGH COOPERATION AMONG PARTICIPANTS

The seven efforts we studied managed natural resource problems that can often cause conflict and controversy, and sometimes litigation. As shown in table 1, the natural resource problems undertaken by the seven efforts we studied ranged widely from fragmented riparian habitat for fish and lack of wildland fire in rangeland ecosystems to predator interactions with livestock, travel access in wilderness areas, and nature-related outdoor activities.

Each of the natural resource problems the efforts managed, or are managing, involves many different interests that can potentially lead to conflict among the different members of the group. For example, in the Blackfoot Challenge case, federal agencies are required to protect threatened and endangered species such as the grizzly bear and the gray wolf, yet ranchers fear these large predators because of the harm they can cause to livestock. Or, in the Uncompahgre Plateau example, as a result of the Energy Policy Act of 2005, transmission line operators must ensure that their power lines remain reliable, which traditionally involved clear cutting the rights-of-ways involved, even on public lands. Meanwhile, natural resource managers seek to provide habitat for lynx and deer and to prevent large openings in the forest that may come with utility corridors. The natural resource problems and potential or actual conflicts managed by each of the groups are described in more detail in appendix II.

As table 1 shows, six of the seven efforts were able to identify solutions to their natural resource problems that met their common interests. For example, by developing the concept of a credit system, the Cooperative Sagebrush Initiative has identified a way to encourage—and pay for—preservation and restoration of sagebrush habitat while also allowing for the development of sagebrush in areas that are economically or otherwise important. In another example, the Onslow Bight Forum identified lands that were important to preserve and restore as habitat for different species and purchased these from willing landowners. Because the groups can pool their funds, they are able to purchase more properties and more expensive properties, and by purchasing the land on the free market from willing owners, the group provides the landowners with the value of their property, thereby not harming their economic interests. While the seventh group—the

Table 1. Natural Resource Problems and Common Interest Solutions of Seven Collaborative Resource Management Efforts

Collaborative resource management effort	Natural resource problem	Common interest solution
Blackfoot Challenge	• Runoff from sawmill into Blackfoot River • Development of private ranches and timberland • Fragmented riparian habitat for fish • Grizzly bear and wolf interaction with livestock • Drought conditions	• Negotiated to keep sawmill in business and to take measures to stop runoff. • Purchased conservation easements to keep land open. Some are managed by state and federal agencies, some by The Nature Conservancy. • Worked with Trout Unlimited to develop a watershed plan for restoring habitat and reconnecting tributaries across private land. • Developed carcass removal program and fencing program for spring calving season. • Wrote water-sharing plan for drought conditions.
Cooperative Sagebrush Initiative	• Managing sagebrush habitat for species at risk, including sage grouse • Expanding the planning scale of sagebrush habitat conservation to address critical habitat areas of key species being affected by permitted development activities	• Developed conceptual plan for sagebrush restoration credits market. • Identified policy assurances that are needed for private landowners to provide habitat for potentially threatened and endangered species. • Solicited pilot projects for restoration of sagebrush habitat.
Eastern Upper Peninsula Partners in Ecosystem Management	• Sustainable ecological management at the landscape scale hindered by lack of cooperation across ownership boundaries • Homogenous (same age and size) forest across landscape that does not provide for wildlife such as neotropical birds	• Developed a common system to classify ecosystem forest types across the eastern Upper Peninsula. • Shared information on ongoing work and projects. As members find common projects, they work on them together.

Table 1. (Continued).

Collaborative resource management effort	Natural resource problem	Common interest solution
Malpai Borderlands Group	• Lack of wildland fire to regenerate grasslands • Effects of fire on threatened and endangered species • Development of open land • Potential overuse of range during drought • Threatened and endangered species habitat on private land	• Developed fire plans with federal agencies to allow wildland fire to be used to manage range vegetation. • Resolved threatened and endangered species issues to allow several burns to occur. Developing habitat conservation plan to allow more burning and protection of species. • Purchased conservation easements to protect ranches from development. • Developed a grassbank to allow ranchers to graze livestock during drought. • Protected the habitat of threatened frogs through drought by trucking in water. Used safe harbor agreement with Fish and Wildlife Service to document habitat requirements on private and nonfederal land.
Onslow Bight Forum	• Development of forest lands and wetlands • Lack of wildland fire to restore habitat and ecosystem Processes • Increase in vehicle/wildlife accidents due to improvements and expansion of transportation system	• Developed plan to identify key areas and habitats for acquisition, restoration, and protection. • Held workshops to discuss using wildland fire to manage native vegetative communities and to identify areas in which to use fire. • Identified opportunities to use wildlife-friendly underpasses during construction of new or improved highways.
Steens Mountain Cooperative Management and Protection Area (CMPA) Advisory Council	• Multiple different management requirements in Steens Mountain CMPA, including travel access in wilderness areas • Juniper encroachment into sagebrush and grasslands	• Provided input on a Cooperative Management Plan to BLM. The plan does not deal with travel access in the area.[a] • Provided recommendations for recreation and juniper management in the area.

Collaborative resource management effort	Natural resource problem	Common interest solution
Uncompahgre Plateau Project	• Homogenous vegetation and lack of understory affecting habitat for mule deer and other species • Power transmission lines and public/private structures threatened by possible wildland fires • Lack of native species for large-scale restoration, rehabilitation, and enhancement projects • Invasive species alter ecology and crowd out native species	• Assessed the condition of vegetation across the Plateau. Identified areas where vegetation could be treated and enhanced and the cumulative effects of such projects, which can be used to assess overall ecosystem conditions. • Identified ways to incorporate vegetation treatments within areas such as utility corridors. • Developed a program to gather and propagate native plants. Developed methods for propagation to transfer to nurseries. • Developed a program to map, monitor, control, and prevent invasive species.

Source: GAO analysis.

[a] BLM completed a travel management plan for the area in November 2007.

Steens Mountain Advisory Council—was able to provide advice on a cooperative management plan and vegetation treatment plans, it did not provide input on a travel management plan for the area, a key management issue.

Steens Mountain Advisory Council

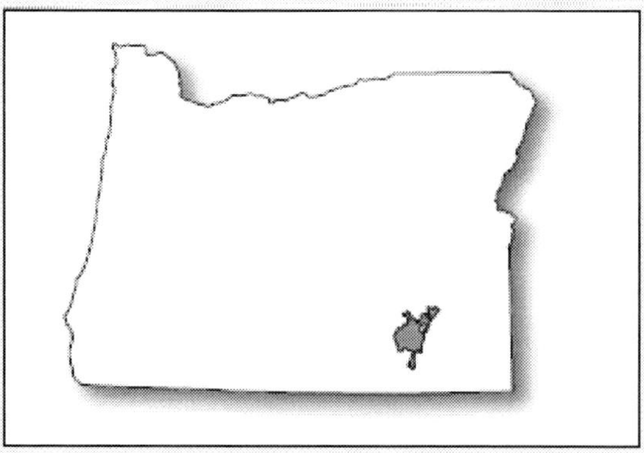

Source: GAO analysis of BLM data.

The Steens Mountain collaborative effort is located in southeastern Oregon. The effort is focused on about 496,000 acres of high desert mountain area that has great ecological diversity and varied wildlife. The primary resource concerns at Steens Mountain include issues related to livestock grazing, wilderness, travel access, and management of junipers that have encroached into sagebrush and grassland areas.

In 2000, the Steens Mountain Cooperative Management and Protection Act established the area and tasked the Steens Mountain Advisory Council with providing innovative and creative suggestions to the BLM on how to manage the natural resources on Steens Mountain in a manner that would alleviate conflict. The Steens Mountain Advisory Council includes local ranchers, recreationists, and environmental representatives.

All seven efforts we studied used several of the collaborative practices identified by the experts—such as seeking inclusive participation; using collaborative processes; pursuing flexibility, openness, and respect; and finding leadership—and six of the efforts were successful in reducing or averting conflicts. These six groups were able to cooperate and focus on their common interests and goals, despite different perspectives and interests among the members. In addition to identifying common goals, several of the successful efforts were able to use other practices, such as obtaining scientific and other information to inform their decisions, leveraging funds, and providing incentives. The one effort that has been less successful in dealing with conflict used several of the collaborative practices, but does not have a common goal and does not have funding to gather information, leverage resources, or provide incentives.

Seek Inclusive Participation

The seven groups each have members that have multiple different perspectives such as private landowners, conservation groups, natural resource land management agencies, and wildlife agencies. Most of the groups include representatives from federal agencies such as BLM, the Forest Service, and the U.S. Fish and Wildlife Service, and several include USDA's Natural Resources Conservation Service. All but one of the groups we studied were primarily organized around landowners and managers who can make decisions about their respective lands, including members of conservation-oriented groups such as The Nature Conservancy and local conservation groups such as the North Carolina Coastal Land Trust and North Carolina Coastal Federation. Two groups, the Blackfoot Challenge and the Malpai Borderlands Group, focus primarily on private lands and the surrounding public lands. On the other hand, the Uncompahgre Plateau, Onslow Bight Forum, and the Eastern Upper Peninsula Partners in Ecosystem Management include large areas of public lands, with the exception of lands owned by the land conservancy groups in North Carolina and several forest companies in Michigan. While the groups are open to other participants such as environmental groups, according to several participants, they may not seek them out or the environmental groups may not participate. All but one of the groups have self-selected membership, which means that they attract members who are interested in working on the problems identified by the group and are willing to find solutions to these problems, which may not be the case with certain organizations. Only one group, the Steens Mountain Advisory Council, is required by law to include certain members, including representatives of the ranching and environmental communities, including one local and one national representative from each.

Develop a Collaborative Process

The seven groups we studied are organized differently but are each organized to collaborate. Three of the groups—the Blackfoot Challenge, the Cooperative Sagebrush Initiative, and the Malpai Borderlands Group—have incorporated as nonprofit organizations, each with a board of directors, and one—the Uncompahgre Plateau Project—has a separate nonprofit financial management group. According to members of one group, being incorporated allows the group the autonomy to raise funds and complete management projects on its own, without relying on the federal or state agencies. Also, incorporating puts the groups on equal footing with the agencies as they identify projects with mutual benefits. Of the remaining three groups, two are less formally organized and one is more formally organized. The Onslow Bight Forum and the Eastern Upper Peninsula group function as information-sharing groups that allow the individual members to determine what actions they will take independently. The Onslow Bight Forum uses a memorandum of understanding to identify the role of each member and the group, while the Eastern Upper Peninsula group does not have any organization documents and operates informally. Finally, the last group—the Steens Mountain Advisory Committee—is a legislatively organized advisory group for BLM and has written protocols to describe its organization and processes.

All but one of these groups uses a consensus process to make decisions. This process involves all participants, focuses on solutions, and proceeds until agreement is reached. For example, participants of one group, the Blackfoot Challenge, said that its members followed the 80-20 rule—they worked on 80 percent of the items they could agree on and left the 20 percent they could not agree on at the door. The participants said that as they worked together longer, the 20 percent of items that cause disagreement have been reduced as well. Two groups—the Onslow Bight Forum and the Eastern Upper Peninsula group—do not make formal decisions, but use a consensus process in discussing and agreeing on a plan of action that members can decide to take or not. One group, the Steens Mountain Advisory Council, uses a voting process to make certain decisions rather than a consensus process. To make a recommendation to BLM, the advisory council is required to have 9 of its 12 members vote in favor of it. According to the members, unfilled positions and poor attendance at council meetings have made it difficult to achieve the number of votes needed to make recommendations to BLM.

Pursue Flexibility, Openness, and Respect

All but one of the groups have flexible and open processes that allow the members to discuss their positions. Two of the groups—the Onslow Bight Forum and the Eastern Upper Peninsula group—would not likely exist without the openness that allowed the members to retain their own missions and land management goals rather than the group subsuming them. Several of the groups, such as the Uncompahgre Plateau Project, use Web sites and plans to communicate with each other and the community. On the other hand, the Steens Mountain Advisory Council is different from the other groups in that it was legislatively created, and the act that created both the Steens Mountain Cooperative Management and Protection Area (CMPA) and the council resulted from lengthy negotiations among several parties, some of whom are, or have been, represented on the council. The group has used facilitators to overcome some of the conflict that developed through the negotiations, but some acknowledge that the council established by the act has not yet resolved key conflicts over management of the area. Yet, some of the members we interviewed were hopeful that a change in members that occurred recently might help to invigorate the group.

Find Leadership

All of the groups have benefited from the availability of community leaders or agency employees who could lead the group. Several of the groups were started by local community leaders who energized and engaged others to work with them, although the federal agency staff were working alongside the community leaders to support the efforts. In particular, the Blackfoot Challenge, Malpai Borderlands Group, and Uncompahgre Plateau projects were started and sustained by community leaders, but they recognize the important contribution of the federal agency employees who were involved as well. On the other hand, federal and state agency employees took the lead in starting the Eastern Upper Peninsula group and were also important in the Cooperative Sagebrush Initiative, and federal agency staff worked with staff from The Nature Conservancy to start the Onslow Bight Forum. One community leader on the Steens advisory council has attempted to focus the group on its role and keep it on track for making recommendations to BLM.

Onslow Bight Conservation Forum

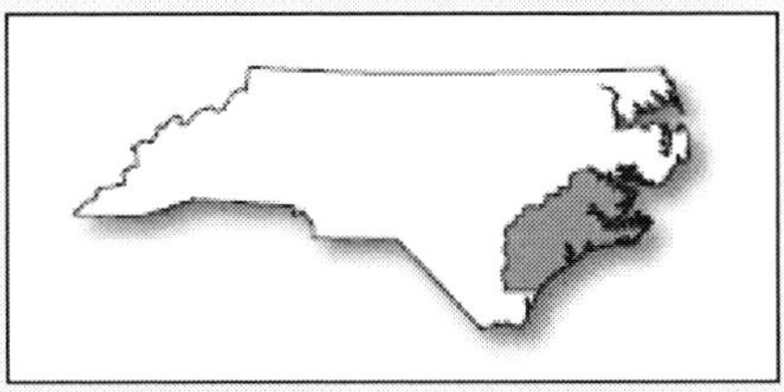

Sources: GAO analysis of The Nature Conservancy data.

The Onslow Bight Conservation Forum is a collaborative group focused on the long-leaf pine forests, estuaries, wetlands, and pocosins (wetlands on a hill that form because of accumulated peat) in coastal North Carolina. The group formed in 2001 around issues such as increasing development and its effects on wildlife habitat, particularly that of the endangered red-cockaded woodpecker, and water quality.

The Onslow Bight Conservation Forum is an information-sharing partnership of federal and state agencies and nonprofit groups who have signed a Memorandum of Understanding to identify opportunities to work together to conserve the natural resources of the Onslow Bight landscape. The members include the Marine Corps, Forest Service, U.S. Fish and Wildlife Service, North Carolina Department of Environment and Natural Resources, North Carolina Wildlife Resources Commission, The Nature Conservancy, the North Carolina Coastal Federation, and the North Carolina Coastal Land Trust.

Identify a Common Goal

Of the seven groups we studied, six identified and shared a common goal. For example, the Onslow Bight Forum brought together diverse members with similar interests in preserving open space and habitat—the

U.S. Marine Corps has an interest in preserving open space around its installations for safety reasons and to help save endangered species, and land conservation groups seek to preserve habitat corridors and prevent development of the rural landscape. Similarly, the Eastern Upper Peninsula group focused on the need to facilitate complementary management of public and private lands, for all appropriate land uses, and to sustain and enhance representative ecosystems in the Eastern Upper Peninsula. On the other hand, the Steens Mountain Advisory Council does not share a common goal for management of the Steens Mountain area, with some members advocating motor vehicle access through wilderness areas for historical uses such as livestock grazing and others advocating for more wilderness areas to be set aside in the planning area and greater conservation requirements instituted in those wilderness areas already existing. The Steens Mountain act established a cooperative management area, the purpose of which is to conserve, protect, and manage the long-term ecological integrity of Steens Mountain for present and future generations. To further this purpose, the act directed BLM to manage the area to achieve five objectives.[8] Several participants indicated that the issue will need to be litigated to clarify the act's requirements.

Develop a Process for Obtaining Common Information

Each of the seven collaborative groups has established a group or process to jointly develop and use scientific information as part of their decision making, although some groups have done so more than others. For example, the Malpai Borderlands Group has a scientific advisory board to develop research projects on fire to support the group's efforts to restore fire, which had been suppressed for decades, to the ecosystem to help restore healthy grasslands. It also holds annual science conferences to bring together the relevant scientific findings on rangelands, fire, threatened and endangered species, and other issues. The group also works with USDA, Forest Service, and university researchers on vegetation and fire studies. On the other hand, rather than develop its own scientific information, the Cooperative Sagebrush Initiative relied on data produced by the U.S. Geological Survey on sagebrush habitat and studies completed by the Western Association of Fish and Wildlife Agencies to assess the status of sage grouse and the sagebrush ecosystem in the 11 western states involved. Several groups developed landscape maps to show different information. For example, the Onslow Bight Forum used habitat and biological information, and other information, to develop a landscape map of the key areas for habitat and preservation purposes. Finally, some groups, such as the Uncompahgre Plateau Project, reported that using scientific information, including field trips to demonstrate effects of their management activities, helped them to communicate their efforts to outside parties who may have otherwise been critical.

Uncompahgre Plateau Project

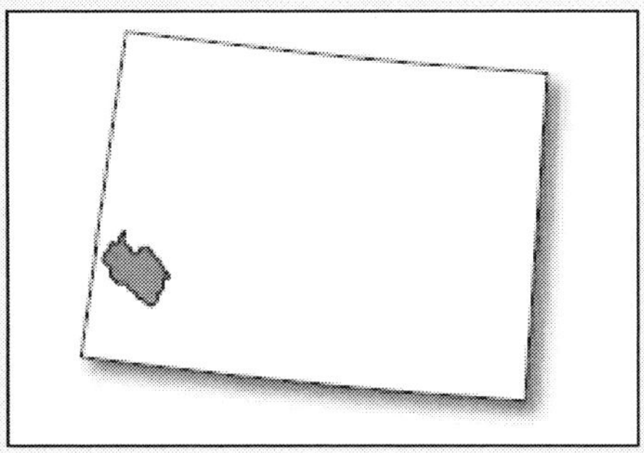

Sources: GAO presentation of Uncompahgre Plateau Project data.

The Uncompahgre Plateau Project collaborative group is located in southwestern Colorado. The group focuses its efforts on the Uncompahgre Plateau, which spans 1.5 million acres, 75 percent of which is public land. The plateau is home to abundant wildlife species, including populations of mule deer. The group formed in 2001 to protect and restore the ecosystem health of the plateau. In addition, key electrical transmission lines that connect the eastern and western United States cross the plateau, creating the need for vegetation management near these lines.

The partners in the Uncompahgre Plateau Project include the Forest Service, BLM, Public Lands Partnership, Colorado Division of Widlife, Western Area Power Administration, and Tri-State Generation and Transmission Association, Inc. The partners signed a Memorandum of Understanding and established an Executive Committee to guide its overall direction; a Technical Committee and contract employees, to carry out its activities; and a nonprofit organization to handle its finances.

Leverage Available Resources

Five of the groups have been able to generate funding from various sources, such as federal and private foundation grants, and to use these funds in conjunction with federal partners' funding to leverage the amount of work that could be done by the group. For example, the Blackfoot Challenge recently received an Ash Institute for Democratic Governance and Innovation[9] award of $100,000, the Uncompahgre Plateau Project received $500,000 from the state of Colorado and $620,000 from the Ford Foundation,[10] and the Malpai Borderlands Group received $8.5 million from its different fundraising efforts. According to the Onslow Bight Forum, its members have raised as much as $75 million since 2001 from state and federal funds to acquire land, a process helped by the existence of the forum. On the other hand, the Eastern Upper Peninsula project and the Steens Mountain Advisory Council do not generate funding. The Eastern Upper Peninsula project members said they did not intend to raise funds because they did not intend to conduct joint projects, and the Steens group is not organized to raise funds. The federal legislation that created the Steens Mountain Advisory Council authorized $25 million to be appropriated to BLM to work with local ranchers, landowners, and others to conduct work in the cooperative management area; however, these funds have not been provided. Some members said that, if provided, these funds could be used to pursue activities such as purchasing private inholdings, which are privately owned lands within the boundary of a national park, forest, or other land management unit.

Provide Incentives

Several of the groups we studied that have dealt successfully with conflict used different types of incentives to gain cooperation and participation. Such incentives include conservation easements, payments for projects or damages caused by wildlife, and different agreements related to threatened and endangered species. The Blackfoot Challenge, Malpai Borderlands Group, and Eastern Upper Peninsula project have arranged, or helped arrange, conservation easements to protect either rangeland or forested land that could have been developed for housing, otherwise. The Malpai group also used another type of payment to help reduce conflict over livestock losses caused by predators, supporting a predation fund to pay ranchers when it can be proved a predator—the jaguar in New Mexico and Arizona—has killed livestock.

Malpai Borderlands Group

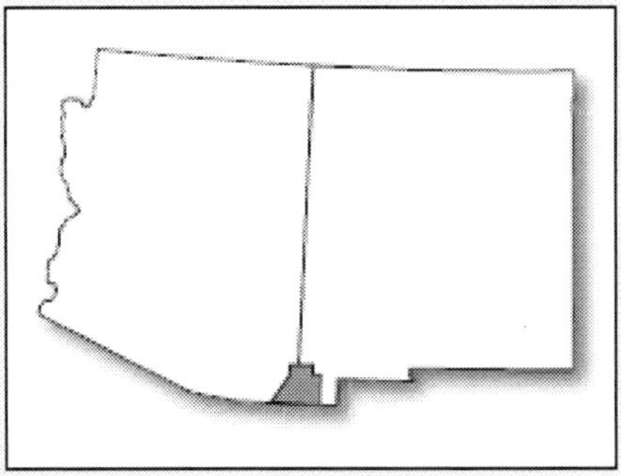

Sources: GAO analysis of Malpai Borderlands Group data.

The Malpai Borderlands Group collaborative effort is located on the border with Mexico in southern New Mexico and Arizona. The group formed a nonprofit organization in 1994 to work on restoring the natural fire regime, preserve large open space, and maintain a rural lifestyle in the approximately 800,000 acres of desert grassland region that includes a mix of federal, state, and private land.

The Malpai Borderlands Group was initiated by a group of ranchers and environmentalists. Federal agencies, including the Forest Service, U.S. Fish and Wildlife Service, and Natural Resources Conservation Service; Arizona and New Mexico state agencies; and conservation groups, such as The Nature Conservancy, have played a role in the group's efforts.

A third type of incentive, safe harbor agreements and habitat conservation plans, has been used by the Malpai Borderlands Group. Safe harbor agreements seek to assure landowners that if they restore or enhance habitat, they will not incur new restrictions if their actions result in a threatened or endangered species taking up residence. In order to obtain a permit to take a species incidental to lawful land management activities, a landowner must complete a habitat conservation plan, which specifies measures the landowner will undertake to minimize and mitigate the effect on the species. These agreements encourage private landowners to conduct projects that will protect species on their property, while also protecting their use of the land should they "take" one of the species—either by killing it or degrading its habitat. According to one group these agreements can be complex and time-consuming to arrange, and thus, it may be more efficient for the group to work with the U.S. Fish and Wildlife Service through the process than for each individual landowner. In addition to these types of arrangements, the Cooperative Sagebrush Initiative wants to develop a related incentive, a conservation credit bank in which one party would pay to protect sagebrush habitat, or conduct restoration of habitat, and another party would purchase credits to develop land that would degrade sagebrush habitat or kill a species. The group is still considering how to measure the conservation value of different sagebrush species and habitat they provide and how to monitor those values.

Collaborative Efforts Have Improved Natural Resource Conditions, but Determining the Extent of Improvement Was Difficult Because of Limited Landscape Data Through cooperating, five of the seven efforts we studied have accomplished multiple management activities and projects that have helped sustain or improve natural resource conditions in their areas. Officials of the five efforts that have completed resource management projects to date said that this work had improved resource conditions and helped to accomplish the goals the groups hoped to achieve. The Cooperative Sagebrush Initiative has not yet accomplished its work, as it started in September 2006 and is just developing demonstration projects. And, although the Steens Mountain Advisory Council has helped BLM to develop a management plan for the Steens Mountain CMPA, it did not deal with the most contentious issues that relate to travel access, wilderness areas, and wilderness study areas in the plan issued in November 2007. Table 2 shows the work accomplished by the different efforts that we studied.

Table 2. Natural Resource Accomplishments, Improvements, and Monitoring by Seven Collaborative Resource Management Efforts

Collaborative resource management effort	Work accomplished	Improved natural resource conditions	Monitoring conducted
Blackfoot Challenge	▪ 90,000 acres of easements acquired ▪ 38 miles on 39 tributaries restored and 62 miles of riparian habitat restored; fish populations increasing ▪ Carcass removal program—340 carcasses removed in 2005; fencing for spring calving ▪ 75 irrigators involved and 60 cubic feet per second of water saved in 2005	▪ Prevent development of private ranches and timberland, maintain open space ▪ Protect riparian habitat, including for endangered bull trout ▪ Limit grizzly bear and wolf conflicts with livestock ▪ Conserve water particularly during drought conditions	▪ Site-specific: Monitoring of riparian projects ▪ Landscape-level: Fish population monitoring in Blackfoot River ▪ Water quality and quantity
Cooperative Sagebrush Initiative	▪ Three ecosystem-scale, integrated projects in development in four states, 1 million acres of sagebrush habitat involved	• Demonstrate ability to manage sagebrush habitat at a large scale for species at risk, including sage grouse	▪ None yet
Eastern Upper Peninsula Partners in Ecosystem Management	▪ Land-type associations created	▪ Create single land-type classification for all lands to facilitate complementary management	▪ None as a group, agency monitoring of various projects, species, and habitat conditions as appropriate

Collaborative resource management effort	Work accomplished	Improved natural resource conditions	Monitoring conducted
Malpai Borderlands Group	▪ 69,000 acres of land burned ▪ Conservation easements protecting 77,000 acres ▪ Grassbank created, allows ranchers to move their cattle during drought to less-affected area ▪ Chiracahua leopard frog habitat protected on private land ▪ In 2007, paid $500 to rancher to compensate for jaguar predation	▪ Reintroduce wildland fire to grasslands ▪ Prevent development of private ranches, maintain open space ▪ Protect lands and financial stability of ranchers ▪ Protect habitat for endangered species	▪ Site-specific: ▪ 290 transects (a sample path) to monitor condition of range in that area ▪ Research project monitoring Species counts before and after projects (such as fires)
Onslow Bight Forum	▪ 57,000 acres of wetlands and other lands acquired, restoration underway ▪ 60,000 acres burned (some as part of regular agency programs)	▪ Acquire lands, protect habitat for endangered species ▪ Acquire lands, prevent loss of open space and restore habitat ▪ Manage wildland fire to restore habitat and ecosystem processes ▪ Use habitat corridors and wildlife-friendly highway underpasses to protect bears and other species	▪ None as a group, agencies monitor projects, species, and habitat conditions as appropriate

Table 2. (Continued)

Collaborative resource management effort	Work accomplished	Improved natural resource conditions	Monitoring conducted
Steens Mountain CMPA Advisory Council	▪ Management plan completed, travel plan completed in November 2007 ▪ Juniper management area with numerous test plots to demonstrate different ways to remove large trees to enable fire to move more naturally through thick juniper stands	▪ Advise on management plan for CMPA ▪ Advise on cooperative management activities in CMPA ▪ Advise on treating juniper encroachment	▪ Monitoring plan for CMPA developed by BLM with review and feedback from the Council
Uncompahgre Plateau Project	▪ Integrated GIS maps and developed plan and projects for two entire watersheds, including BLM and Forest Service land ▪ Treated 50,000 acres of agency land ▪ Gathered native seeds for more than 50 plants and developed methods for propagating these ▪ Treated invasive species on more than 100,000 acres	▪ Restore wildlife habitat on the Plateau ▪ Reduce vegetation to reduce fire threats ▪ Develop native seed program to provide vegetation conditioned to the area ▪ Reduce invasive species on public and private lands	▪ Site-level: Condition of vegetation in project areas after treatment ▪ Landscape-level: Location of vegetation treatments and burns to show overall openings and continuity of trees and vegetation

Source: GAO analysis.

As shown in table 2, the efforts' accomplishments ranged widely, from developing joint plans and scientific information, to changing vegetation conditions and managing species habitat. For example, some of the groups developed landscape maps of vegetation and potential habitat that integrated information for each of the members in the group. The groups also accomplished numerous activities to keep landscapes open and usable for natural resource purposes, such as grazing or timber harvesting. At the same time, the groups worked on several projects to help conserve threatened and endangered species habitat. The two efforts that have not completed projects—the Cooperative Sagebrush Initiative and the Steens Mountain Advisory Council—have not moved beyond planning work.

As shown in table 2, three of the groups—the Blackfoot Challenge, Malpai Borderlands Group, and Uncompahgre Plateau Project—have employed monitoring programs that demonstrate the effect of their activities on site-level natural resource conditions. Monitoring environmental or natural resource characteristics is typically conducted at the site level—the area involved in a management activity, such as a vegetation treatment—to determine what effect the management activity has, or at the landscape level—a broad area—to determine the overall conditions across that area. Monitoring can also be conducted over time to indicate the trend in conditions at a site or landscape. Montana's Department of Fish, Wildlife and Parks, one of the partners involved in the Blackfoot Challenge, conducts fish surveys in the Blackfoot River to determine how populations are faring. This work measures the benefits provided by the group's riparian projects for fish populations, including endangered bull trout. The Malpai Borderlands Group conducts range monitoring on 290 sites in its area and conducts monitoring of some species to determine how they have been affected by group projects. The Uncompahgre Plateau Project maps its vegetation treatments and fires, and thus shows areas of different vegetation ages, types, and the habitat it provides across the broad area managed by several agencies. Because the agencies' mapping data are not compatible, however, staff said that they had to develop ways to merge the data, which was is time-consuming and expensive. Through January 2008, the agencies, with the help of the group, had pulled together data for two large watersheds and had begun working on two more. The other groups do not conduct monitoring as a group, although the resource management agencies do track resources in some cases.

Two of the seven groups—Blackfoot Challenge and the Uncompahgre Plateau Project—monitor the results of some of their projects across the larger landscape to determine the effect of their work across the broad landscapes that they are trying to affect; however, the other groups do not conduct landscape monitoring. According to two groups, they are not able to monitor across a larger area for two primary reasons. First, according to participants, it is time-consuming and expensive to monitor multiple sites regularly across a large area, and this is what is necessary to understand the effects of multiple projects in that large landscape. For example, even though the Malpai Borderlands Group monitors 290 sites for the effects of grazing, climate, and other factors on the condition of the grasslands that are useful for assessing the condition of that pasture or smaller area, according to the group's scientists, the group does not collect comparable data across different pastures or smaller areas that allow comparison across the broader landscape. Data must be collected at a different, broader scale and need to be collected consistently at specified locations to determine the condition of the hundreds of thousands of acres of rangeland that the group is helping to manage. Currently, the group and its scientific advisory board are considering what data to collect.

The second reason that the groups do not collect data is that they either have not agreed to collect such data or they have not agreed on the work that they will conduct and monitor. Two groups—the Onslow Bight Forum and the Eastern Upper Peninsula group—do not monitor because both of these groups organized to share information, not to develop joint projects and monitoring. According to some Onslow Bight members, it would be useful to track the results that individual members have accomplished with the group's information, but the group has not decided to do this jointly or to dedicate the resources to it. According to the members of the Eastern Upper Peninsula group, their purpose has never been to jointly manage projects and therefore there is no need to monitor results. The group's purpose is to share information about natural resource problems, such as invasive species, and effective ways to treat them, without requiring the participants to work together. The group gives members a place to find common problems with other agencies and then each agency or participant can conduct its work and monitor results accordingly.

Finally, the Cooperative Sagebrush Initiative and the Steens Mountain Advisory Council do not conduct any monitoring because the groups are just beginning projects that warrant monitoring. The Cooperative Sagebrush Initiative recognizes the need for monitoring and has considered including the cost of monitoring in each project to ensure that it is conducted, but the group has not yet conducted any projects, nor have they conducted pilot projects to ensure that they can correctly measure the benefits achieved by restoration projects. At Steens Mountain, BLM has drafted an overall monitoring plan for the Steens Mountain area that may serve to monitor work accomplished. However, BLM has not yet conducted some of the key work identified as needed by the Advisory Council because the agency is still conducting studies to determine how to best clear juniper in wilderness areas and wilderness study areas because mechanical tools—the method that has been proven effective for removing large juniper trees—cannot be used to cut down trees prior to burning.

Chapter 5

COOPERATIVE CONSERVATION POLICIES AND ACTIONS ADDRESS SOME OF THE CHALLENGES FACED BY FEDERAL AGENCIES PARTICIPATING IN COLLABORATIVE EFFORTS, BUT OPPORTUNITIES EXIST FOR FURTHER ACTION

Federal land and resource management agencies face several challenges to participating in collaborative resource management efforts, according to the experts, federal officials, and participants in collaborative efforts we interviewed. Key challenges that the agencies face include improving federal employees' collaborative skills and working within the framework of existing laws and policies. The 2004 Executive Order and 2005 White House Conference on Cooperative Conservation set in motion an interagency initiative, including a senior policy group, an executive task force, and working groups, to develop policies and take actions that support collaborative efforts and partnerships. The policies and actions taken as part of the initiative have made progress in addressing the challenges agencies face. However, additional opportunities exist to develop tools, examples, and guidance that would strengthen federal participation in collaborative efforts and better structure and direct the Cooperative Conservation initiative to achieve its vision.

Federal Land and Resource Management Agencies Face Several Challenges to Their Participation in Collaborative Resource Management Efforts

As the federal land and resource management agencies work to collaborate with state, local, private, and tribal entities, they face several challenges. The key challenges identified by experts, federal officials, and participants in collaborative efforts we interviewed include (1) improving federal employees' collaborative skills; (2) determining whether to participate in a particular collaborative effort; (3) sustaining federal employees' participation over time; (4) measuring participation and monitoring results to ensure accountability; (5) sharing agency and group experiences with collaboration; and (6) working within the framework of federal statutes and agency policies to support collaboration.

Improving Federal Employees' Collaborative Skills

The first challenge agencies face involves improving their employees' skills in collaboration, as well as increasing their use. Such skills include improving communication, identifying and involving relevant stakeholders, conducting meetings, resolving disputes, and sharing technical information and making it accessible. Federal participants and others we interviewed indicated that federal employees are often technical experts and improving their collaborative skills may enable them to work more effectively with a collaborative group. They indicated that such skills are important to work effectively with neighboring landowners and community members who are interested in the projects and lands. Many participants emphasized that hiring new people with collaborative skills is one way to improve the level of collaboration by federal agencies and also said that training in collaboration for employees is important to improve skills. Some federal agency officials said that hands-on training in collaborative efforts, involving participants from other groups, is most helpful.

Furthermore, to encourage the use of collaboration by federal employees, several participants we interviewed said that management should support field staff in their collaborative efforts. For example, one participant stated that management needs to identify those employees with collaborative skills and assign them according to these skills. Some participants said that senior employees may be better at collaboration because they have developed a relationship with the group or are more comfortable in interpreting laws and policy to apply in specific situations that might arise. Others said that new employees have enthusiasm and only need to be shown how they can best work with groups. Several participants said that federal agencies need to allow their staff to become acquainted with a community to work better with local groups, and others said that providing flexibility for the employees to work with the groups is needed. Finally, one participant we interviewed said that collaborative efforts will fail if federal management officials reverse the decisions made by the federal representatives working with a collaborative group because the group will no longer trust the federal agencies to do what they have agreed on.

Determining Whether to Participate in a Particular Collaborative Effort

A second challenge agencies face in working with collaborative groups is determining whether or not to participate in a particular group. Collaborative efforts are commonly started by concerned citizens interested in the management of their public lands and, as a result, the federal agencies can choose whether to be involved and what role to play. If they make an uninformed choice, they risk becoming involved in a group that might take great effort and expend considerable staff resources with few results. Various external factors affect a collaborative group's ability to cooperate and succeed, including a community's collaborative capacity and the amount of controversy involved. If federal agencies do not understand these contributing factors, as well as the nature of the controversy related to a problem, federal staff may become involved in a collaborative effort that has little chance of working, potentially leading to increased conflict and costs.

Part of determining whether to be involved is what role the agencies can play. Participants we interviewed indicated that it is important for federal agencies to be involved in collaborative efforts because they are such large landowners, and, in many areas, natural resource problems cross their boundaries onto other lands. However, several participants—including federal agency officials—indicated that the agencies should "lead from behind," letting the group take a lead in determining what work can be done. One participant said that by doing this, the community works out their issues and comes to a common understanding among themselves—without the agency staff brokering the discussion. In such cases, the agencies can help the groups by providing planning assistance, technical information, funding, and even administrative support. In other cases, the federal agencies may want to use a collaborative group to provide input on a management plan or project, and in these cases, the agencies need to determine which groups to involve and what their particular natural resource management concerns are. Regardless of the federal role in collaboration, experts and participants emphasized the need for federal agencies to clarify how a group's agreed-upon ideas could affect decisions about federal land.

Sustaining Federal Participation over Time

Once federal staff have become involved in a collaborative effort, a third challenge becomes sustaining employees' participation over time. This is particularly important because of limited resources available in the field offices and the staff's limited ability to participate while also conducting their work for the agency. Experts and participants we interviewed said that, to be effective, federal participation should be consistent and ongoing throughout the collaboration, which can be for many years. For example, participants of the Blackfoot Challenge and the Malpai Borderlands Group indicated that their groups had benefited from agency staff acting as liaisons to the groups for several years. These groups were highly organized in their efforts and worked with agency officials to create these relationships. However, at many of the field offices we visited, federal agencies were experiencing staffing limitations that made their work with existing collaborative efforts more difficult and limited. In particular, the federal agencies' field offices had experienced recent downsizing in the last several years and were one or two people below their normal staffing levels. As a result, the remaining staff members were spread thinly across existing programs to accomplish their work and achieve targets set by the agencies. According to the officials, these federal employees sometimes continued to participate in collaborative efforts but devoted less time and attention to them. For example, in North Carolina, federal officials for the National Park Service, U.S. Fish and Wildlife Service refuge, and Forest Service had been involved in the Onslow Bight Forum efforts to map key habitat, but as their biologists left the agencies, the agencies became less involved and attended fewer meetings.

Another issue related to staffing and federal agency support of collaborative efforts is the agencies' practice of transferring people frequently from one field location to another. Participants said that longevity and a "sense of place"—or commitment to an area—is important for collaborating with groups whose participants may have been in an area for generations. A few participants thought that changing staff helped to bring in new people with energy and new ideas, but, according to several other participants, moving staff frequently creates a gap in the support for a group, which may hinder progress if a federal participant for a project moves at the wrong time. Some participants thought that the transition between outgoing and new federal staff could be eased by the outgoing staff member writing a memo to describe all the relevant details of the group, its members, its issues, and its projects, among other things, but others thought that it would be better to rely on the other staff in the office or group members for knowledge about the group, community, and other factors that would affect the agency's participation.

Measuring Participation and Monitoring Results to Ensure Accountability

Once a collaborative effort has begun, an important challenge faced by federal agencies and the members of the group is measuring participation and monitoring the results of the efforts. Measurement and monitoring allow members, both federal and nonfederal, to be accountable to each other and to the public. In the case of the federal agencies, measuring participation and monitoring results help show how an agency's participation in a group has helped to achieve some important resource management goal for the agency. According to federal officials we interviewed, agencies will be involved in collaborative efforts to the extent that the group can help them achieve federal land management goals and targets for work they are required to do. However, according to experts, federal officials, and participants, it is difficult to measure the results of collaboration because there is no direct measure or "widget" produced from participating or collaboration. For example, according to one participant, counting the number of meetings held does not measure collaboration, and, in fact, the number of meetings needed for a well-run group may decrease over time. Participants also said that it may take a few years to build a group and relationships before any work is accomplished, which may not fit with agency performance targets that are set annually.

Moreover, experts said that monitoring the natural resources results of collaborative management is also difficult because of the long-term nature of ecological change. For example, it can take several years before the results of a management project can be seen or measured; at the same time, natural fluctuation in drought, vegetation, and species can mask the effects of management actions. To counter these difficulties, according to some participants we interviewed, groups need to have an overall plan for the improvements in natural resources they are working to achieve and monitor according to those goals. Even then, as the examples we studied show, collaborative groups have a difficult time monitoring because of the time and cost involved.

Sharing Agency and Group Experiences with Collaboration

A fifth challenge that the federal agencies face in participating in collaborative efforts involves sharing agency and group experiences with collaboration. By their nature, collaborative groups are decentralized and localized, with their members focused on the group's management plans and activities. According to experts and participants, these groups are each unique in their makeup, organization, circumstances, and abilities, yet can experience similar problems working together and with federal agencies. Some participants who had been involved in the White House Conference on Cooperative Conservation and other conferences stated that such forums are useful for giving groups the opportunity to share practical experiences of working together and with federal agencies. The types of lessons include the fact that groups can benefit from paid staff, even part-time, or a director to keep the group organized between meetings.

Working within the Framework of Federal Statutes and Agency Policies to Support Collaboration

Finally, agencies face the challenge of collaborating within the existing framework of federal statutes and agency policies that establish a management culture within each agency. In addition to the framework of natural resources and environmental laws and policies described above, agencies have a set of laws and policies for working with nonfederal entities or groups, including the Federal Advisory Committee Act, policies on ethics related to working with groups, and financial assistance requirements. Some experts and participants in collaborative groups identified aspects of federal laws and agency policies as being inconsistent with collaboration. However, aspects of the policies reflect processes established to support good government practices such as transparency and accountability. The federal agencies have not, in all cases, evaluated the laws and policies involved to determine how best to balance collaboration with the need to maintain good government practices. A short description of these laws and policies follows.

Federal Advisory Committee Act: Some experts and collaborative groups assert that the Federal Advisory Committee Act inhibits collaborative management by imposing several requirements on interaction between federal and nonfederal participants. For example, the act requires that all committees have a charter, and that each charter contain specific information, including the committee's scope and objectives, a description of duties, the period of time necessary to carry out its purposes, the estimated operating costs, and the number and frequency of meetings. The act generally requires that agencies announce committee meetings ahead of time and give notice to interested parties about such meetings. With some exceptions, the meetings are to be open to the public, and agencies are to prepare meeting minutes and make them available to interested parties.[11] By making the process bureaucratic, some experts and others say that the act limits groups' abilities to work together spontaneously to solve problems or get work done. USDA officials indicated that they have a budget limit on what they can spend on groups working under the act. Some participants of collaborative groups we interviewed said that the fact that the act's requirements do not apply to privately led efforts is one reason for communities to lead collaborative efforts with assistance from federal agencies. Other participants said that the act's requirements caused their groups to focus their goals solely on information sharing, because the group's purpose would not be to offer advice regarding agency decisions, and therefore the group would not be subject to the act.

Ethics rule: USDA and Interior implement federal ethics' rules on federal employees' participation on the board of directors of an outside organization differently, resulting in their staff members participating in different capacities on a group's nonprofit board. The ethics rules generally prevent a federal employee from serving as a board member while serving in an official capacity for the federal agency because of concerns over conflicts of interest. Waivers may be granted under limited circumstances; however, according to USDA and Interior officials, USDA rarely grants waivers, while Interior has granted some waivers. As a result of different implementation of the rule, in the Blackfoot Challenge case, a Forest Service member serves as a nonvoting board member, while BLM and the U.S. Fish and Wildlife Service members serve as voting members. Several of the participants of the group expressed confusion and some distrust over the different federal agency interpretations, saying that they raised some questions about the Forest Service's commitment to participate. Other groups that form nonprofit boards may face this same inconsistency.

Financial requirements: Some groups receive federal grants or cooperative agreements that enable them to conduct activities that provide for a public purpose. Nonfederal participants in collaborative efforts identified federal agency financial procedures for these grants and cooperative agreements that make it difficult for them to work collaboratively with the agencies. For example, some grants require that any interest earned be returned to the federal government, others require the group to raise funds to meet a share of costs, or others do not allow the group to be paid up front, which is difficult for small organizations without much funding. In addition, several participants indicated that it is difficult to pull together funding over the long term from the numerous sources available—foundations, agencies, and fundraising activities—and that this is an ongoing struggle for groups. However, because federal agencies need to seek competing offers or applications for many types of grants and agreements, the agencies may not be able to provide stable funding to groups for very long. For example, the participants of one group we interviewed recently learned that they would have to compete with others to renew their agreement, even though the group has ongoing management plans and projects with BLM and other agencies to provide long-term vegetation management across the agencies' lands. The result of this action is that the group was uncertain if they would be able to carry out these long-term plans and projects because they rely on this stream of funding to pay for part-time staff to organize the group and provide support for planning projects and reporting the results.

One specific type of funding agreement that can help make collaboration work, identified by some federal officials we interviewed, is the watershed restoration and enhancement agreement. Under this authority the Forest Service can use appropriated funds to enter into agreements with other federal agencies; states, tribal, and local governments; or private entities to protect, restore, and enhance fish and wildlife habitat and other resources on public or private land. However, the authority that allows this for the Forest Service—the Wyden Amendment—is set to expire in 2011.[12] In addition, Interior officials stated that they do not have general authority to use their funds to restore or enhance resources on nonfederal land; however, they indicated that BLM, the U.S. Fish and Wildlife Service, and the National Park Service can fund projects on nonfederal land related to reducing the risk of damage from wildland fire. The agency officials that discussed these funding sources said that the ability to spend some of their funds on nonfederal lands enhances—or would enhance—their ability to work with partners in the community.

Endangered Species Act requirements for listing species: Participants in the Cooperative Sagebrush Initiative identified several aspects of the Endangered Species Act that make collaboration difficult for them. They have identified and proposed areas where they believe Endangered Species Act policies could be made more consistent with their collaborative effort. In particular, the group is planning to conduct restoration projects for sagebrush habitat, but, according to one participant, these restoration projects are scrutinized as much as a destructive project is in terms of the effect the project may have on a potentially endangered species such as the sage grouse. The group has proposed to Interior that the policy for listing species as endangered—the Policy for Evaluating Conservation Efforts—would apply to their restoration actions because such actions might make listing unnecessary, or listing requirements might be less restrictive. This policy identifies criteria the U.S. Fish and Wildlife Service will use in determining whether formalized conservation efforts that have yet to be implemented or to show effectiveness contribute to making listing a species as threatened or endangered unnecessary. The group has also proposed other changes to the Endangered Species Act regulations and policies that they say would support collaboration and their particular effort. For example, under current policies, the U.S. Fish and Wildlife Service treats the two types of species (threatened and endangered) in the same manner with regard to prohibitions on the taking of a species. The group has proposed that Interior relax the prohibition on the taking of threatened species, arguing that the Endangered Species Act allows for threatened species to be treated in a different manner from endangered species.

National Environmental Policy Act: Experts and participants have stated that NEPA hinders collaboration by essentially duplicating the public participation that occurs through collaborative efforts. Collaborative groups may develop a plan or project that they would prefer. For federal projects having a significant environmental effect, NEPA requires the development and analysis of a reasonable range of alternative actions, including the agency's preferred alternative action, in an environmental impact statement. It also requires public participation in the development of the environmental impact statement. Because collaborative groups often include many of those interested in the natural resources or management being conducted, several participants said that the collaborative group provides the agencies with its preferred alternative and a good sense of the public's opinion of the project.

They believe, for this reason, that NEPA requirements are redundant in these cases.

Cooperative conservation policies and actions have made progress in addressing the challenges agencies face, but additional opportunities exist to strengthen federal participation in collaborative efforts building on the agencies' earlier efforts to develop their partnership programs and abilities to work collaboratively; the 2004 Executive Order and 2005 White House Conference heightened attention to partnerships and collaboration across the federal government. After the White House Conference, a report entitled *Supplemental Analysis of Day Two Facilitated Discussion Sessions* (Day 2 report) was written summarizing the comments of numerous participants in collaborative groups and highlighting actions that the federal agencies could take to improve cooperation and partnerships.[13] In response to the Day 2 report, a senior policy team—composed of the Chairman of CEQ, Director of OMB, and selected Deputy Secretaries of the departments—identified issues to be further addressed by an executive task force and working groups.[14] The task force formed—or incorporated—working groups to address several overall themes identified in the Day 2 report: personnel competencies, training and development, legal authorities for cooperative conservation, conflict resolution, the Federal Advisory Committee Act, education, federal financial assistance, measuring and monitoring, volunteers, engaging the public, and Web site development. Table 3 shows the challenges we identified with input from experts, federal officials, and participants in our review; proposed actions from the Day 2 report that are responsive to the challenges; and the policies or actions taken by the task force working groups that address the challenge.

As shown in table 3, several actions have been taken, including development of policies, that have resulted in progress toward addressing several of the challenges agencies face participating in collaborative efforts, but other opportunities exist to take actions that further address the challenges.

Table 3. Cooperative Conservation Actions, Proposed and Initiated, That Can Address Challenges Federal Agencies Face in Collaborating

Challenge	Day 2 report proposed actions to implement Cooperative Conservation	Cooperative Conservation working group actions
Improving employees' collaborative skills	▪ Assess personnel policies and hiring practices to ensure that staff members possess good communication and collaborative skills; train agency staff in collaboration and skills associated with establishing and maintaining partnerships and integrate skills into leadership and management training programs. ▪ Increase capacity to use joint fact-finding approaches that involve stakeholders in the development of questions; teach scientists how to communicate and problem solve with groups. ▪ Ensure personnel hiring, promotion, and reward policies provide incentives for collaboration, problem-solving, and risk-taking.	▪ The personnel competencies working group developed competencies for agencies to consider as part of human capital policy. Agencies have developed human capital policies that discuss hiring and rewarding collaboration. ▪ The training and development working group reviewed and organized training programs for all agencies to identify those that include collaboration and make them widely available. ▪ OMB and CEQ issued guidance on collaborative problem-solving principles based on a report by an interagency task force convened by the U.S. Institute for Environmental Conflict Resolution.
Determining whether federal agencies should participate	None.	None.
Sustaining federal participation over time	None.	None.

Table 3. (Continued).

Challenge	Day 2 report proposed actions to implement Cooperative Conservation	Cooperative Conservation working group actions
Measuring participation and monitoring results	▪ Create an interagency task force to develop project monitoring protocols and final project evaluation. ▪ Develop and implement effective measures of progress and look for opportunities to address cooperative conservation in agency performance measures.	▪ The measuring and monitoring working group gathered and analyzed different tools to help groups demonstrate the leveraging effect of partnerships and collaboration. Some of these tools can help groups monitor their results.
Sharing agency and group experiences with collaboration	▪ Communicate success stories and lessons learned and capture and publish best management practices. ▪ Work with other people engaged in cooperative conservation to create models and "how to" guidance about communicating risk and scientific information to citizens. ▪ Facilitate the development of a network of people familiar with cooperative conservation. ▪ Organize and support annual conservation conferences and regional cooperative conservation conferences.	▪ The Web site working group developed the Cooperative Conservation Web site, which includes lessons learned and examples of collaboration. Cooperative Conservation America also publishes examples online. ▪ The Collaborative Action Team, including members of national nonprofits, created the Western Collaboration Assistance Network (WestCAN) that seeks to broaden the community of people working together on public lands issues. It provides technical assistance, best practices, lessons learned, and mentoring services.

Challenge	Day 2 report proposed actions to implement Cooperative Conservation	Cooperative Conservation working group actions
Working within legal and cultural framework	▪ Assess existing legal incentives and disincentives that can influence collaborative efforts, including the Federal Advisory Committee Act, NEPA, and the Endangered Species Act. ▪ Analyze agency procedures for grants and contracting to remove barriers to partnerships and landscape-level management and collaboration. ▪ Create incentives, processes, and policies to communicate across fragmented agencies to overcome boundaries between agencies and programs. ▪ Review personnel policies that move staff frequently.	▪ The Legislative working group, with agencies, prepared legal primers on agencies' authorities to collaborate. ▪ The Federal Advisory Committee Act working group is working on streamlining internal procedures, providing consistent legal advice, and other actions, but is not done. ▪ The Federal financial assistance working group has delegated this task to departments.

Source: GAO analysis.

The challenge of improving federal employees' collaborative skills is being addressed by the personnel competencies working group. Through 2007, with the input of the Office of Personnel Management, this working group developed a set of collaborative behaviors for federal employees that some of the agencies have made part of their strategies to hire and train employees to improve their collaborative skills. According to Interior and Forest Service officials, senior executive service managers in the agencies are already rated on their ability to collaborate and collaborative behaviors. Interior agencies are now considering how to incorporate these into personnel rating systems for other federal officials and staff, and the Forest Service has revised its employee rating system and incorporated the collaborative competencies into the new system for both managers and employees. In addition, the training and development working group identified and published appropriate training courses offered by each of the land and resource management agencies. For example, BLM and the Forest Service offer a series of courses that include collaborative behavior, and BLM offers one course that visits a community and trains community and agency members on how to work as a group.[15] According to a member of the working group, the idea of an experience-based training, in which staff would visit and work with an experienced group, has been developed but none of the agencies have adopted this at the time of our review. Furthermore, in 2005, CEQ and OMB issued joint guidance, developed by a broad interagency task force convened by the U.S. Institute for Environmental Conflict Resolution, to encourage agencies to use collaborative problem-solving and elaborate on the principles of collaboration.[16] According to officials, the institute also offers a series of courses on collaboration that federal agencies can take.

The twin challenges of determining (1) whether to participate in a particular collaborative effort and (2) how to sustain federal employees' participation over time have not been addressed by policies or actions of the task force or its working groups. However, BLM published a collaborative guidebook in 2007 that includes a discussion of factors to consider in determining whether to collaborate. Similarly, the Forest Service's Web site links to various partnership assessment tools created by the Natural Resources Conservation Service and private companies. In addition, the Forest Service developed an assessment document that guides an office through an analysis of its workload and how much time it can devote to a collaborative effort. The results of this analysis can help determine whether an office will be able to sustain their participation in a group. Finally, the Forest Service has adopted a tool developed with the Collaborative Action

Team, called a transition memo, which allows an employee transferring locations to leave detailed documentation about the community, groups, leaders, and other information for the person coming into the position. While these separate tools are available to the individual agency that developed them, they have not been shared or adopted more broadly among the federal agencies to help them in making decisions whether and how much to participate in particular collaborative efforts. Without tools to assess these aspects of collaboration, particularly as the agencies increase their ability and efforts to participate in collaborative efforts, agencies may be more likely to get involved in unsuccessful efforts.

The challenge of measuring participation and monitoring results of collaborative efforts, as shown in table 3, has been partly addressed by the measuring and monitoring working group. Through September 2007, the working group gathered, reviewed, and analyzed tools that measure and monitor how cooperative conservation activities help achieve environmental protection and natural resource management goals. For example, the working group discussed different means to demonstrate the leveraging power of partnerships and collaboration. Some of these tools can also help people engaged in partnerships and collaborative efforts monitor how they are doing and improve their efforts during the process. In addition, the working group identified a few resources that discuss, in general, monitoring of natural resource conditions. In October 2007, the group posted a variety of tools on the Cooperative Conservation Web site, which is an initial step to address this challenge.[17] However, actions that would more fully address natural resource monitoring—the Day 2 report indicated that project monitoring protocols would be useful—have not been taken by the task force or working groups. CEQ officials indicated that an ongoing effort on key national indicators might help to address this aspect of the challenge. However, until guidance or protocols on natural resource monitoring for collaborative groups is provided, federal agencies and groups will be unable to track and relate their progress to Congress, the communities, or other interested parties.

The challenge of sharing experiences among agencies and groups has been partly addressed through the actions of the outreach working group, which has developed an official Web site and examples of collaborative experiences. In addition, in 2007, the Collaborative Action Team started WestCAN, facilitating the development of a network of people familiar with cooperative conservation. Other actions identified in the Day 2 report that could be taken and would address this challenge include organizing and the supporting annual conservation conferences. As of October 2007, the agencies had held nationwide listening sessions, but had not held or proposed any further conferences on cooperative conservation either nationally or regionally. Federal officials indicated that such meetings can be expensive and time-consuming to organize and that they would like others to take the lead in organizing them. They also indicated that it is important to have clear goals and objectives for such meetings and that the meetings should lead progressively to achieving these goals and objectives. Individual agencies have held conferences in the past; they also meet regularly with nonprofits interested in the collaborative approach through the Collaborative Action Team. However, these meetings and tools may not provide the opportunity for the different agencies and groups to meet and share information and possible solutions, or the face-to-face experiences that participants in the conference found valuable. Without such meetings, it would be difficult for the groups to be able to meet periodically to generate ideas and share information or develop a cooperative conservation network.

The challenge of working within the agencies' legal framework is being addressed, as shown in table 3, by several actions. At a broad level, the legal authorities working group worked with the agencies to publish a compendium, for each department, of the authorities that allow and support collaboration, which will help agency staff who are working with collaborative groups to understand the requirements that they face. More specifically, the status of actions to resolve perceived inconsistencies between the authorities and collaboration include the following:

- The Federal Advisory Committee Act working group is streamlining requirements for federal advisory groups, which is one of the primary pieces of legislation that agencies and participants in collaborative efforts have identified as inconsistent with collaboration. According to CEQ officials, the Federal Advisory Committee Act team has determined that flexibility exists within the current law and policy for groups and is developing the best way to share this information with agency staff and group participants, such as training.
- A legal analysis of the incentives and disincentives affecting collaborative groups—particularly those associated with the Endangered Species Act and NEPA—was an action proposed by the Day 2 report that has not been addressed by the task force or working groups. In addition, USDA's and Interior's different implementation of ethics rules resulted in inconsistent decisions regarding federal employees serving on nonprofit boards. While no specific actions have been taken by the task force, Interior is

evaluating regulatory and policy changes to the Endangered Species Act in response to the concerns raised during listening sessions held in 2006, and by the Cooperative Sagebrush Initiative. As of October 2007, Interior had not proposed any regulatory or policy changes to the Endangered Species Act. Also, in October 2007, CEQ issued guidance on collaboration within the NEPA process that discusses using a collaborative group's option as the preferred alternative in a NEPA analysis.[16] The guidance resulted from the recommendation of a federal task force in 2003 and followed the issuance in 2005 of a report by the National Environmental Conflict Resolution Advisory Committee concluding that one way to achieve NEPA goals is for the federal agencies to use environmental conflict resolution practices, including collaboration.[18] However, no evaluation or action has occurred as of October 2007 to resolve the inconsistent application by USDA and Interior of federal ethics rules.

While these actions are addressing the Federal Advisory Committee Act, Endangered Species Act, and NEPA, the federal financial assistance working group did not complete its task of evaluating the extent to which cooperative funding authorities could be enhanced to better assist collaboration. Because of the number and complexity of funding authorities, the working group determined that each department should undertake an analysis of its own financial assistance to collaborative groups. Through December 2007, Interior was considering its use of cooperative agreements and whether they can be used to support partners to conduct work that is mutually beneficial to the group and Interior agencies. In such situations, both the partners and the federal agencies bring resources to the table and both sides benefit from the work jointly conducted. However, an Interior official noted that the laws related to federal contracting may limit the agencies' ability to use these agreements in the absence of specific statutory authority to do so.[19] In September 2007, an Interior official stated that the type of authority needed is reflected in authorities provided to the Natural Resources Conservation Service and other agencies that allow them to work with partners on mutually beneficial activities. Through September 2007, the Forest Service had authority to use cooperative agreements with private and public organizations, including nonprofit groups, to perform the forestry protection activities and other types of cooperative projects that provide mutual benefits, other than monetary considerations, to both parties.

In addition, the agency has authority to work on the mutually beneficial restoration projects under the Watershed Enhancement and Restoration Act or Wyden authority, but this authority is not permanent, extending only to 2011.

In late December 2007, Congress passed, and the President signed, the Consolidated Appropriations Act for the fiscal year 2008, which included two provisions related to agencies and cooperative agreements. The first provision authorizes Interior to enter into cooperative agreements with state or local governments, or not-for-profit organizations, if the agreement will (1) serve a mutual interest of parties to the agreement in carrying out Interior's programs and (2) all parties will contribute resources. The second provision extended through 2010 the Forest Service's authority to enter into cooperative agreements with state, local, and nonprofit groups if agreement serves the mutual benefit (other than monetary consideration) of parties carrying out programs administered by the Forest Services and all parties contribute resources. However, the overall problem of facilitating collaborative partnership projects for collaborative groups and partners—in terms of interest, cost share, and other administrative matters—remains. For this reason, an overall evaluation of federal funding assistance and tools available for collaborative groups could help identify situations across agencies that hinder collaboration and potential legal and policy changes that could be made.

Overall, the working groups and agencies have made some progress in developing policies and taking actions that address the challenges they face in working with collaborative groups. However, these challenges will not be fully addressed or solved in the short term. As indicated in the Day 2 report, the actions to be taken by federal agencies would require a sustained effort and a senior policy team with an overall strategy to sequence the many actions that need to be taken by multiple different federal agencies. While the Cooperative Conservation initiative is being coordinated by a task force and working groups, both are temporary, formed by federal agency personnel interested in the cooperative approach but who, for the most part, have other full-time responsibilities. Because of this, the structure and direction—which includes goals, actions, time frames, and responsibilities—of the initiative as it moves forward are uncertain. According to CEQ and agency officials, the task force working groups were organized to propose actions that could be taken in the short term; CEQ officials said that the senior policy team would meet to assess the status of actions and progress toward the vision laid out for the Cooperative Conservation initiative. As of December 2007, the policy team had not met, but CEQ officials expected they would meet after the issuance of the second annual report on the implementation of the Cooperative Conservation initiative. Currently, the task force is developing the report, which was expected to be issued in January 2008.

Chapter 6

CONCLUSIONS

Collaborative resource management offers federal land and resource management agencies a promising tool with which to approach the ongoing and potential conflicts that arise in managing the nation's land and resources. Compared with the alternatives—such as litigation or individual landowners making independent, potentially conflicting decisions about their separate parcels of land—collaboration provides groups a way to integrate multiple interests and achieve common goals. To date, federal land and resource management agencies have had some success in working with collaborative efforts. Moreover, the policies put in place through the Cooperative Conservation initiative move the federal government and agencies forward in supporting collaborative resource management efforts. However, based on the challenges that the agencies face in working with collaborative efforts, additional opportunities exist to enhance and effectively manage federal agencies' participation in and support of ongoing and future collaborative efforts. Specifically, because federal agencies have limited resources and time, yet at the same time have multiple opportunities to collaborate, they need to be judicious in their decisions about collaborating with particular efforts and could benefit from guidance on how this can be done. This would involve dissemination of tools that already exist for field offices to assess a community's capacity for collaborating, and the federal ability to participate. In addition, because the agencies are accountable to Congress and the public for achieving their land and resource management goals, it is important for them to be able to demonstrate the results that have been accomplished through collaborative efforts. This means that agencies and groups should be able to measure participation and monitor their progress, including monitoring the broader landscape-level effects that result from their collaborative efforts and projects.

Furthermore, collaborative resource management is just beginning to emerge as one approach for federal land and resource agencies to work with local groups in ways that can reduce conflict and improve resources.

In addition to developing capability among agency personnel, federal agency support for this approach entails helping to create networks, identifying best practices, and generating new ideas. These outcomes can be achieved though facilitating the exchange of information and lessons learned among collaborative groups, as was done at the White House Conference. Federal support also involves an ongoing commitment to identify practicable legal and policy changes that could enhance collaboration. In particular, CEQ, OMB, and other federal agencies can evaluate and identify possible changes to federal financial assistance authorities and policies that make it difficult to work with partners. Also, USDA and Interior can identify a way to achieve more consistent results in determining participation by USDA and Interior employees on nonprofit boards. In the future, as the agencies participate in different collaborative efforts, additional situations may arise in which agencies need to seek ways to implement laws or policies in a manner that enhances collaboration.

Finally, because collaborative resource management involves multiple departments and agencies facing common challenges and will take a sustained effort to implement, it is important that the effort has structure and long-term direction to ensure that it is ongoing and completed. Structure could be provided by continuing such an interagency effort as the Cooperative Conservation task force and its working groups. One way this could be accomplished would be by developing a memorandum of understanding between participating agencies. Long-term direction to address common challenges could be provided by the memorandum of understanding, or through another organizational document or plan that will steer the task force, working groups, and agencies toward realizing the vision of the initiative.

Appendix I

OBJECTIVES, SCOPE, AND METHODOLOGY

The objectives for this study were to determine (1) experts' views of collaborative resource management as an approach for addressing complex natural resource management problems; (2) the extent to which selected collaborative resource management efforts have addressed land use conflicts and improved natural resource conditions; and (3) what challenges, if any, federal land and resource management agencies face in participating in collaborative resource management efforts and how the Cooperative Conservation initiative has addressed the challenges.

For the first objective, to determine experts' views of collaborative resource management as an approach for addressing natural resource problems, we examined the academic literature related to the topic. To identify relevant articles in the literature, we first interviewed experts who have studied collaborative resource management. Following GAO's methodology for identifying experts, we started with knowledgeable individuals and agency personnel and asked them for referrals to experts. In an iterative process, we contacted these experts and asked them for nominations of other knowledgeable individuals. We interviewed over 20 individuals who could be considered experts, based on the nominations of others in the field. We asked these experts for references to articles on the collaborative resource management approach. We also identified articles through a search of four academic databases including Agricola, a database of articles relating to aspects of agriculture, forestry, and animal science; ProQuest Science Journals, a database of science and technology journals that includes literature on biology and earth science; ECO, a database of scholarly journals; and BasicBIOSIS, a database of biology and other life science-related journals. We searched these databases using the terms "ecosystem management policy" and "collaborative resource management policy," which produced over 950 articles in the four databases. Abstracts of these articles were reviewed and only those articles appropriate for our work were retained for a literature review. This process yielded over 130 articles (the full article was used, not just the abstract).

To perform the literature review, one of two analysts (A, B) read and reviewed each of the articles and indicated whether or not the contents included themes related to our objectives, that is, the common practices, benefits, limitations, and critiques of collaboration. The analysts summarized information from the articles that was relevant to these themes and recorded it as statements in a database. To verify that the two analysts were extracting similar information from the articles, the analysts randomly selected 10 percent (13) of the total articles. For each of these 13 articles, if Analyst A had originally summarized and categorized relevant information in the article, then Analyst B independently performed the same tasks. Similarly, Analyst A reviewed the articles originally reviewed by Analyst B. For each article, the verification work was compared with the original and it was determined whether both analysts agreed or disagreed on the presence of information in the article related to each theme. This analysis indicated that the two analysts were extracting comparable information from the articles.

A content analysis was then performed on the statements. Each analyst classified the statements from the articles read as a benefit, limitation, or critique associated with collaborative resource management. The analysts then exchanged data and examined the other analyst's categorizations to determine whether there was agreement on classifying each statement from the literature review into the benefits, limitations, and critiques categories. The two analysts reviewed the statements they had placed into these categories and either concurred with the classification or noted the basis of disagreement. For items where there was disagreement, the disagreement was resolved so that agreement was 100 percent.

Once the analysts had established a unified set of statements under each category—benefits, limitations, and critiques—each analyst independently grouped the statements under each category into similar components. The analysts' lists of components for each category were compared, discussed, and merged into one set. The components we agreed upon for each category and a description of them are noted in table 4.

Table 4. Description of the Benefits, Limitations, and Critiques of Collaboration

Components	Description
Category: Benefits	
Reduction in Conflict and Litigation	Conflict is reduced and better managed, which may prevent parties resorting to litigation.
Better Natural Resource Results	More creative solutions are identified and better decisions are made because a broad array of knowledge, including local information, is incorporated into decisions. Solutions are easier to implement because there is typically less opposition, sometimes leading to a cost savings.
Shared Ownership and Authority	Ownership and responsibility for a problem are shared and state and federal agencies become partners with local agencies and groups. Such joint stewardship can make federal and state programs more locally relevant and can increases fairness in the process.
Increased Trust	Increased trust among participants, between organizations, and between decision makers.
Improved Communication	Communication is improved and becomes more open and honest.
Increased Understanding	Participants learn about and gain an understanding and appreciation of the natural resource problem and of other participants' perspectives, including local knowledge.
Increased Community Capacity	Increased community capacity involves increased public engagement and awareness, social networks, and community ability to engage in dialogue.
Category: Limitations	
Process Difficult/Time-Consuming	The process can be inefficient, slow, and require large amounts of resources.
Process Does Not Always Work	There are circumstances in which collaboration or reaching consensus is not possible for reasons such as irreconcilable differences, particular groups derailing the process, or a resistance to change.
Category: Critiques	
Process Is Not Equitable	Power is not equally balanced among participants, placing some at a disadvantage and making the process undemocratic. Not all groups who have a legitimate interest may be able to participate, which may mean that their concerns are not addressed. For example, national environmental groups cannot participate in all local efforts.

Table 4. (Continued).

Components	Description
Category: Benefits	
Results in One, or More, Groups Being Co-opted	The collaborative group is taken over or assimilated by a more powerful or established interest.
May Produce Least Common Denominator	The focus on consensus as an end result can lead to a solution that is a compromise that may not necessarily reflect the best science or the view of any group.
Reduced Accountability	Lessened accountability to the public or individual constituencies occurs through aspects of the process such as devolving federal authority to collaborative groups and removing discussion from the public eye.

Source: GAO analysis.

After developing the categories and components, we independently assigned each of the statements to one of the components. After the statements were independently assigned a component, the analysts discussed every statement for which they had assigned different components and reached agreement on the category for each of the statements. As a result, the analysts attained 100 percent agreement on the assignment of statements to components. Table 5 reports the number of statements that were assigned to each component.

Table 5. Number of Statements in the Components of Each Category

Components	Number of statements
Benefits	
Better Natural Resource Results	31
Shared Ownership and Authority	21
Increased Understanding	14
Increased Community Capacity	12
Reduction in Conflict and Litigation	11
Increased Trust	6
Increased Communication	5
Limitations	
Process Does Not Always Work	18
Process Difficult/Time-Consuming	14
Critiques	
Reduced Accountability	26
Process Is Not Equitable	23
Results in One, or More, Groups Being Co-opted	18
May Produce Least Common Denominator	9

Source: GAO analysis.

The literature review was also used to identify what the experts viewed as common practices of successful collaborative groups. Such practices were described in 15 of the articles from the literature review and one GAO report that described practices to sustain collaborative efforts among federal agencies.[1] To develop a comprehensive list to summarize the practices described in all of these sources, two analysts independently generated lists based on commonalities of those described in the literature. A third analyst reconciled the two lists and all three analysts discussed the results and agreed on the following final list of practices:

- Seek inclusive representation.
- Develop collaborative processes.
- Pursue flexibility, openness, and respect.
- Establish leadership.
- Identify or develop a common goal.
- Develop a process for obtaining information.
- Leverage available resources.
- Provide incentives.
- Monitor results for accountability.

For the second objective, to determine the extent to which selected efforts have addressed land use conflicts and improved natural resource conditions, we identified seven examples involving collaborative resource management efforts. The examples were identified using referrals made by experts and citations in the literature. The seven examples we chose to study were judgmentally selected based on several criteria, as shown in table 6, designed to capture groups with (1) a significant amount of federal land involved, (2) participation of multiple stakeholders, (3) locations across the United States, and (4) different types of groups, from nonprofit groups, to an advisory council, to loosely organized information-sharing groups. Although there are many collaborative efforts dealing with water issues, we confined our examples to land management efforts to limit the scope of our work. The examples we selected included both new and experienced groups, made up of multiple participants including federal agencies, from rural areas. The groups chosen and the states in which they are located are shown in table 6.

To gather information on each group's organization, efforts, and results, we conducted field visits and detailed, semistructured interviews with several key participants of the group, and in some cases, interested parties who were not participating in the group. We obtained related documentation of each group's activities and results and in some instances observed the groups' projects in the field. We did not independently verify data related to the groups' results. In analyzing the groups, we considered conflicts to exist if two or more participants had different interests to achieve and considered conflicts to be reduced or averted if a common solution or interest was identified.

Table 6. Collaborative Resource Management Groups Selected as Case Examples

Collaborative effort	Year group started	Location	Approximate acres of land involved (federal lands involved)	Group type	Stakeholders
Blackfoot Challenge	1993	West-central Montana	1.5 million acres (Lolo and Helena National Forests, Bureau of Land Management [BLM] land)	Nonprofit organization	Forest Service, BLM, U.S. Fish and Wildlife Service, state and local agencies, businesses, foundations, nonprofit organizations, private landowners, schools, communities
Cooperative Sagebrush Initiative	2006	11 western states	(Federal land in the western United States)	Nonprofit organization	U.S. Fish and Wildlife Service, BLM, Natural Resources Conservation Service, U.S. Geological Survey, nonprofit organizations, energy companies, private landowners
Eastern Upper Peninsula Partners in Ecosystem Management	1992	Eastern Upper Peninsula of Michigan	4 million acres (Hiawatha National Forest, Seney National Wildlife Refuge, Pictured Rocks National Lakeshore)	Information-sharing	Forest Service, National Park Service, U.S. Fish and Wildlife Service, a state agency, a nonprofit organization, and companies owning private forest land

Table 6. (Continued).

Collaborative effort	Year group started	Location	Approximate acres of land involved (federal lands involved)	Group type	Stakeholders
Malpai Borderlands Group	1994	Southern Arizona and New Mexico	800,000 acres (Coronado National Forest, BLM land, San Bernardino National Wildlife Refuge)	Nonprofit organization	Forest Service, BLM, Natural Resources Conservation Service, U.S. Fish and Wildlife Service, state agencies, nonprofit organizations, private landowners
Onslow Bight Conservation Forum	2001	Coastal North Carolina	(Marine Corps Base Camp Lejune, Marine Corps Air Station Cherry Point, Croatan National Forest)	Memorandum of understanding, information-sharing	Department of Defense, Forest Service, U.S. Fish and Wildlife Service, state agencies, nonprofit organizations
Steens Mountain Advisory Council	2000	Southeastern Oregon	496,000 acres (Steens Mountain Cooperative Management and Protection Area)	Legislatively created advisory council	BLM, nonprofit organizations, recreationists, private landowners
Uncompahgre Plateau Project	2001	Southwestern Colorado	1.5 million acres (Grand Mesa, Uncompahgre, and Gunnison National Forest; BLM land)	Memorandum of understanding	BLM, Forest Service, a state agency, a community group, electric utilities

Source: GAO analysis.

For the third objective, we identified challenges associated with the collaborative resource management approach described by the experts in the literature and by members of the collaborative resource management groups we studied. The components of the challenges described by the experts in the literature were identified using the literature review and content analysis that is explained above. Table 7 describes the challenges.

Table 7. Description of the Challenges Associated with Collaboration Identified by the Experts

Challenge	Description
Improving Federal Employees' Collaborative Skills	Skill and experience interacting and communicating with the public and conflict resolution skills.
Determining Whether to Participate in a Collaborative Effort	Evaluating particular factors that will affect whether a collaborative effort is likely to succeed in a particular circumstance. Such factors include the capacity for the community to engage in such efforts, which may depend on the community having leaders, social networks, and local infrastructure and institutions that facilitate civic involvement; and external conditional factors that may include an issue that has a history of litigation and viewpoints rooted in the community that participants bring with them into a collaborative effort such as stereotypes or a history of distrust among community members.
Sustaining Participation	Achieving and sustaining the consistent participation of all relevant stakeholders and people with collaborative, leadership, and technical skills and being able to build trust and equal footing among the participants. Also includes a lack of sufficient time, money, or people to fully support a collaborative effort.
Measuring and Monitoring for Accountability	Achieving and demonstrating accountability through measuring participation and monitoring natural resources given the long time horizons of natural resource results.
Working within Federal Laws and Agency Policies	Agency support of collaboration through culture, funding, laws, and policies, and relationships with other agencies and organizations.

Source: GAO analysis.

As with the benefits, limitations, and critiques, each statement identified as a challenge in the literature review was assigned to a component. The number of statements that were assigned to each challenge component is listed in table 8.

Table 8. Number of Statements in the Challenges

▪ Challenge	▪ Number of statements
▪ Sustaining Participation	▪ 58
▪ Determining Whether to Participate in a Collaborative Effort	▪ 49
▪ Working within Federal Laws and Agency Policies	▪ 35
▪ Measuring and Monitoring for Accountability	▪ 21
▪ Improving Federal Employees' Collaborative Skills	▪ 10

Source: GAO analysis.

An additional challenge related to sharing experiences with collaboration was identified through semistructured interviews with collaborative group participants. Many participants we interviewed mentioned that aspects of their collaborative group were unique, yet the groups share similar problems and could benefit from sharing experiences with other groups. This challenge reflects the personal experiences of participants working within a specific collaborative group.

To identify how efforts under the Cooperative Conservation initiative address challenges associated with federal land and resource management agencies' participation in collaborative resource management, we interviewed federal officials from organizations responsible for implementing the Cooperative Conservation initiative, including the Council on Environmental Quality, Office of Management and Budget, Department of the Interior, and Department of Agriculture. In addition, we reviewed Cooperative Conservation documents and agency guidance related to partnerships and Cooperative Conservation.

We conducted this performance audit from October 2006 through February 2008, in accordance with generally accepted government auditing standards. Those standards require that we plan and perform the audit to obtain sufficient, appropriate evidence to provide a reasonable basis for our findings and conclusions based on our audit objectives. We believe that the evidence obtained provides a reasonable basis for our findings and conclusions based on our audit objectives.

Appendix II

Collaborative Resource Management Groups and Successful Collaboration Practices

To understand the purpose and nature of collaborative resource management groups, we selected seven such groups for detailed study. We met with participants of these groups individually or, at times, together to discuss the natural resource problems and conflicts the group was managing and the practices used by the group that enabled them to successfully alleviate conflict and improve resource conditions. To various degrees, the seven groups we studied used the collaborative practices identified by experts that successful groups commonly use. Experts emphasized that while these practices are commonly used by successful groups, the use of these practices does not guarantee success for all groups. Collaborative groups are unique and can succeed or fail depending on the nature of the problem or conflict involved. The following describes each of the collaborative groups, the natural resource problems or conflicts they managed, and the extent to which they used collaborative practices.

Blackfoot Challenge

The Blackfoot Challenge (Challenge) is a landowner-based nonprofit group working in the 1.5-million-acre Blackfoot River watershed in Montana. Although it began much earlier, the group was officially established as a nonprofit group in the early 1990s, with a board including private landowners and federal and state agency personnel.[1] The participants of the group sought to create an organization that could resolve natural resource issues, such as the reintroduction of threatened and endangered species and their effect on private landowner livelihoods, before they became conflicts.

Of the total acres in the watershed, about 57 percent is publicly managed by the Forest Service, Bureau of Land Management (BLM), and the state of Montana. The remaining lands in the watershed are owned by timber companies and private citizens. The area has had a long history of mining, logging, and ranching. More recently, the area has increasing numbers of people, which has increased development and recreation. The ecosystem is also home to threatened and endangered species including the bull trout, grizzly bear, and gray wolf.

Natural Resource Problems

Participants of the Challenge identified several natural resource problems and conflicts that the group has managed, and is continuing to manage, including the following:

- In 2000, the Challenge responded to a conflict that arose over low water flows in the Blackfoot River that threatened the survival of fish and other river species and organisms. The Challenge formed a Drought Response Committee, which has since expanded to address long-term water conservation and recreation issues. The committee met with the Big Blackfoot Chapter of Trout Unlimited, which had concerns about fish populations and habitat; Montana Department of Fish, Wildlife and Parks; and water users to develop an emergency drought plan for the river. The plan, based on the idea of "shared sacrifice," provided more in-stream flow as water users voluntarily reduced the amount of water they withdrew, allowing more water to be left in the stream. In 2005, this plan helped save 60 cubic feet per second of water.[2]
- Riparian habitat for fish in the Blackfoot River is fragmented by culverts, roads, and other infrastructure on both public and private land that block tributaries and creeks flowing into the river. Wildlife agencies have noticed the reduction in fish populations, including the threatened bull trout. Many groups, including federal agencies, fishermen and women, and ranchers, are interested in reconnecting streams that have been blocked to provide better fishing and

wildlife habitat opportunities. However, some ranchers are hesitant about making improvements or working with federal agencies. The group has worked with willing ranchers and the local chapter of Trout Unlimited to develop a plan for restoring riparian areas and tributaries across the watershed. Over time, the groups have protected and restored 38 miles on 39 tributaries and 62 miles of riparian habitat.

- In 2002, the Challenge responded to concerns throughout the valley about increased grizzly bear activity by creating a Wildlife Committee to exchange information and coordinate efforts. The Blackfoot watershed is nearby three wilderness areas and is considered a prime wildlife corridor for wolves and grizzly bears, whose populations are increasing. Local landowners are concerned about increased human and livestock interaction with such species. The Challenge began a Carcass Pick-Up Program in conjunction with the Montana Department of Fish, Wildlife and Parks; the U.S. Fish and Wildlife Partners Program; local ranchers; and a waste service to remove dead livestock from ranches to deter bears from searching for such remains. Human-grizzly bear conflicts have been reduced by 91 percent from 2003 through 2006.
- In 2005 and 2006, the Challenge dealt with two unique resource conflicts. In the first case, conflict arose over a housing development around one particular community in the watershed that would dramatically affect an important elk migration corridor and increase the community's population, water use, and school enrollment. As a result, there were many different stakeholders interested in the issue. Rather than taking a position on the conflict, the Challenge has instead brought the community together with the stakeholders to find an acceptable alternative. In a second similar case, members of the Challenge did not take sides on a controversial proposed gold mine near Lincoln, Montana, in the northern part of the watershed. Instead of advocating for a particular solution, the Challenge offered to bring people together to discuss their options. In the end, according to the participants, the state passed a law against methods of mining that use cyanide to leach the gold from the rocks and the proposed mine was ultimately blocked.

Collaborative Practices

The collaborative practices used by the Challenge are described in the following sections.

Seek Inclusive Representation

The Challenge board and its working committees include a wide variety of representation. Members of the board are landowners, land managers, agencies, and others who are represented through working committees and membership. The group has tried to involve every type of stakeholder in the process to provide help or share resources. They realize, however, that some perspectives that should be included may be missing from the board, including absentee landowners who own second homes in the valley. In an effort to provide greater inclusiveness, the board has created at-large members.

As members of the Challenge, federal agency officials are members of the Executive Board and committees. Because the Challenge provides a forum for information sharing, agency officials have an opportunity to hear community concerns. It allows them to know, in an informal capacity, if local people are supportive of particular actions before making decisions.

Of equal importance, the agencies have an opportunity to communicate correct facts about their respective agencies. This helps to correct rumors and reduce doubt, uncertainty, and distrust between the community and the agencies and provides a forum for agency officials to make participants aware of their limitations early in the process. Although federal employees serve as members of the Executive Board, a nonprofit board, the Forest Service member serves as a nonvoting member, while the BLM and U.S. Fish and Wildlife Service employees serve as voting members.

Develop a Collaborative Process

The group uses an "80-20" rule, whereby the group concentrates its efforts on 80 percent of the issues it can agree upon and does not force consensus on the 20 percent that it is unable to agree upon. This strategic approach allows the group to first work on solutions to problems that are less controversial and more likely to succeed, thereby building common ground and trust among participants. The Challenge does not advocate any one position because it believes if it did, it would be unable to act as a bridge between two sides of an issue. Instead the group chooses to facilitate dialogue and information sharing. This process helps to promote community dialogue between private landowners and public agencies in an attempt to resolve issues before they become major conflicts.

Pursue Flexibility, Openness, and Respect

Members of the Challenge attributed much of their success as a group to the time they have taken to develop trust among members. Participants of the Challenge include individuals that are respectful of diverse views, committed to the effort, and are willing to negotiate and build consensus. One member described the group's common approach as polite, thoughtful, kind, and respectful.

Find Leadership

According to participants, a collaborative group needs the right leader and the Challenge has had several committed, talented community leaders over the years. They view the right leader as someone who is a local opinion leader and who has the respect of a majority of the community. A participant described one of the reasons for the Challenge's success as inspired leadership, which involves being able to focus the group on its common interests. The group also hired an Executive Director, which was a crucial step for the Challenge in terms of raising funds and organizing the group because it could only accomplish a limited amount on a volunteer basis.

Identify a Common Goal

Concern for maintaining a certain quality of life in the area prompted landowners, public agencies, and other community leaders to begin working together on ways to manage the watershed. The group's mission is to "coordinate efforts that will enhance, conserve and protect the natural resources and rural lifestyles of Montana's Blackfoot River Valley for present and future generations." As early as the 1970s, private landowners and public agency officials worked together to resolve conflicts, or potential conflicts, among various users within the watershed. For example, in an effort to protect and restore fish and wildlife habitat along the river corridor, several public agencies, including BLM, the Forest Service, U.S. Fish and Wildlife Service, and state wildlife and parks agencies, attempted to purchase conservation easements from private landowners. The landowners made the agencies aware that they were each asking to acquire land, and the agencies and landowners started talking about their common goals. In the 1980s, a conflict over access to the river between recreationists and private riparian landowners developed. To access the river, recreationists had to trespass on private lands.[3] In response, a local timber company joined with BLM and the Montana Department of Fish, Wildlife and Parks to allow limited access across private land to use the river if the agencies would manage the activities and effects on resources.

Develop a Process for Obtaining Information

The Challenge relies on the scientific expertise and information provided by the resource managers from the federal and state agencies. To make decisions about specific resource management problems, the group has a standard set of committees that include knowledgeable agency and community members. One committee in particular, the Drought, Water Conservation, and Recreation committee, monitors snowpack, stream flow, and drought conditions, as well as recreation use of the river. The Challenge has recently become involved in monitoring and developing water quality standards for streams in the watershed because the water quality data needed to analyze and improve conditions in the watershed were inadequate. It also works with university researchers to conduct studies.

Leverage Available Resources

In the past, the Challenge has operated on about $50,000 per year, receiving funding from private donors and foundations. The group recently received a $100,000 award for innovations in governance from the Ash Institute for Democratic Governance and Innovation at Harvard University. The group's resources are used to leverage federal funds by coordinating private projects with federal projects. For example, as the Forest Service and BLM work to restore parts of a stream on their respective lands, the Challenge coordinates the projects and adds its own resources to conduct work on private stretches of the same stream, thereby providing greater stream restoration than if the agencies had conducted individual projects.

Provide Incentives

The Blackfoot Valley uses conservation easements as an incentive for conservation activities. Through many partners, more than 100 conservation easements on more than 90,000 acres of private lands have been purchased to keep agricultural and grasslands open and available for ranching and wildlife use. Conservation easements are being purchased and donated to the following organizations: Forest Service; U.S. Fish and Wildlife Service; Montana Fish, Wildlife and Parks; The Nature Conservancy; Montana Land Reliance; and Five Valleys Land Trust.

Monitor Results for Accountability

For the most part, the Challenge uses monitoring data that the agencies collect, although in specific cases, the group and its partners are monitoring the results of their projects. In particular, the local chapter of Trout Unlimited led the development of a process to prioritize tributaries and stretches of the river to restore and monitor results. In addition, the Montana Department of Fish, Wildlife and Parks monitors fish populations in the river, which indicates habitat improvement and water quality conditions. The Challenge recently began monitoring water quality.

COOPERATIVE SAGEBRUSH INITIATIVE

The Cooperative Sagebrush Initiative (Initiative) is a partnership of landowners, communities, local working groups, conservation groups, industries, and tribal, state, and federal agencies that started in 2006 to focus on conservation of the western sagebrush landscape. The effort encompasses the sagebrush range, which spans 11 western states, and involves creating incentives for conservation through mechanisms such as a system to trade credits for conservation activities.[4] The group incorporated into a nonprofit organization in 2007 and is still organizing and planning the effort, so it has not yet conducted conservation activities. In 2007, the group solicited proposals for projects designed to demonstrate how the work could be done and incentives could be developed and has endorsed three proposed projects that encompass over 1 million acres of sagebrush habitat in four states.

In the mid-1990s, the declining status of two sage grouse species—Gunnison sage grouse and greater sage grouse—triggered regional concern for the health of the sagebrush ecosystem. In 2000, the Gunnison sage grouse was added to the U.S. Fish and Wildlife Service's list of candidate species to be considered for a threatened or endangered listing under the Endangered Species Act and the greater sage grouse was the subject of three petitions in 2002–2003 seeking listing throughout its range. The U.S. Fish and Wildlife Service found that a listing was not warranted for the greater sage grouse in 2005, or for the Gunnison sage grouse in 2006. The sagebrush range is also home to wildlife, such as mule deer, valued for hunting; scenic attractions; energy resources; and ranching; which could be affected by declining greater sage grouse populations or a listing of one, or more, of the species that are dependent on the sagebrush ecosystem.

Natural Resource Problems

The primary natural resource problem that the Initiative is focused on is the decline of the sagebrush range and associated decline in greater sage grouse populations. These declines have been attributed to factors such as increased oil and gas exploration and development in the West, some ranching practices, and climate. Although the sage grouse species were not listed when originally petitioned, there are three lawsuits that could affect the legal status of the sage grouse.[5] The states, energy companies, ranchers, and developers are concerned that a listing decision would limit their activities in sagebrush habitat.

Collaborative Practices

The collaborative practices used by the Initiative are described in the following sections.

Seek Inclusive Representation

The Initiative was started when representatives of a nonprofit organization called the Sand County Foundation saw an opportunity for oil and gas companies to become involved in stewardship of the sagebrush ecosystem and help with key issues hindering sage grouse conservation in the West that were identified in a report sponsored by the Western Association of Fish and Wildlife Agencies. These key issues included creating an organizational structure for conservation efforts, establishing leadership to coordinate the efforts, and finding resources to fund the efforts. Representatives from the Sand County Foundation and the U.S. Fish and Wildlife Service initiated discussions with representatives from BLM, the U.S. Geological Survey, and Encana Oil and Gas to develop ideas for a collaborative conservation effort that spanned the range of the sage grouse.

The partners believe that the effort should be broad, inclusive, and representative and, therefore, include key state agencies; counties; tribes; a wide spectrum of landowners, ranchers, and citizens; a diverse mix of companies across multiple industries; a good representation of local, regional, and national conservation groups; and other federal agencies such as the Department of Defense. Potential partners in the Initiative were identified through conversations among the core group who initiated the effort. Subsequently, invitations to participate were sent out broadly to individuals and the list of potential partners grew through further recommendations. At the second major general meeting of the group in December 2006, over 80 people attended, including representatives from federal and state agencies, energy companies, and nongovernmental organizations, as well as private landowners.

After its initial efforts to gain participation, the Initiative formed a partnership and outreach working group responsible for identifying and communicating with critical partners for the Initiative, as well as developing an outreach strategy to inform key audiences of the Initiative's purpose and achievements. Partners we spoke with noted that they believe they have good representation from all of the necessary interests, although some noted that the tribes have not been involved thus far even though they have been encouraged to participate.

Develop a Collaborative Process

Decisions within the Initiative are made by consensus and meetings are facilitated by a staff member from the U.S. Institute for Environmental Conflict Resolution. To accomplish work, the Initiative has developed a strategic plan that includes four working groups: (1) a partnership and outreach group to ensure that the Initiative includes all stakeholders and reaches out to underrepresented interests; (2) an incentives group to work on incentive mechanisms for the participants; (3) a projects group that identifies and prioritizes conservation projects; and (4) a funding group that is developing a banking structure for the group.

The Initiative is governed by a 12-member Partnership Council that includes representatives from the Cooperative Sagebrush Steppe Restoration Initiative, Encana Oil and Gas, EnerCrest Corporation, Environmental Defense, Idaho Cattle Association, Idaho Department of Fish and Game, National Cattleman's Beef Association, Peabody Energy/Powder River Coal, Shell Oil, Western Governor's Association, Sand County Foundation, Utah Department of Natural Resources, Vermillion Ranch, and Western Association of Fish and Wildlife Agencies. In addition, there are nonvoting federal advisory members on the Partnership Council from the U.S. Geological Survey, U.S. Fish and Wildlife Service, and Natural Resources Conservation Service.

Pursue Flexibility, Openness, and Respect

According to some of the partners, the group views transparency as the best way to deal with critics and skeptics and, therefore, has invited everyone to participate. By having an open process for discussion, the group has been able to respectfully discuss different perspectives even though the members do not always agree. As one participant described it, there is more to the process than sitting around singing "kumbaya." In addition, the group posts most of its information and documents on its Web site and opens its meetings and conference calls to any stakeholders who want to participate.

Find Leadership

Several participants attribute the initial success of the group to the visionary leadership of some of the group's founders who saw an opportunity for conservation in the concurrent trends of increased oil and gas development in the West and decreasing sagebrush habitat. One of the participants noted that the group has benefited from several different leaders who have the ability to share a vision with others and motivate them to work toward it by focusing on problem solving and solutions.

Identify a Common Goal

The Initiative partners came together around the goal of conserving sagebrush habitat, with the focus on preventing the need for a listing of the greater sage grouse under the Endangered Species Act. The partners have identified a common goal which is to "result in the long-term, verifiable recovery of the greater sage grouse and improvement of other species of concern in the sagebrush range." Some participants noted that the Initiative would not exist without the threat of a listing because each of the partners has different concerns over the need for or result of a listing. For example, conservation organizations want to maintain the health of the species, industry is concerned over increased limitations on energy exploration and development in sagebrush habitat that would be brought about by a listing, and ranchers are concerned that a listing would restrict their activities on their private land as well as on the public land associated with grazing leases.

Develop a Process for Obtaining Information

The Initiative has utilized the expertise of scientists from the state wildlife agencies and the federal agencies to guide various aspects of the effort and has used existing sagebrush habitat data from the U.S. Geological Survey and sage grouse conservation studies completed by the Western Association of Fish and Wildlife Agencies across the 11-state sage grouse range. In 2006, a panel of sage grouse scientists, representing 10 state wildlife agencies, the U.S. Fish and Wildlife Service, BLM, Natural Resources Conservation Service, and the Forest Service convened to identify priority areas of conservation and types of conservation efforts that would benefit the sagebrush range. In addition, to mentor applicants who have applied for conservation projects under the Initiative and help them develop the details of their project, one of the working groups has been charged with recruiting a Science Advisory Council that will consist of scientists with expertise in sage grouse biology, range management, landscape ecology, and conservation biology. Furthermore, in February of 2007, the Initiative sponsored a workshop to explore how a conservation credit trading system for the sagebrush ecosystem may be defined. This workshop brought together sage grouse and sagebrush scientists as well as experts familiar with other credit trading systems such as wetland banking programs, endangered species conservation banks, and carbon offset programs.

Leverage Available Resources

The Initiative's early efforts have been funded by some of the member organizations such as the Sand County Foundation,[6] National Fish and Wildlife Foundation, and Encana Oil and Gas. The funds generated thus far have paid for meetings and planning activities, but participants anticipate that the Initiative will be able to raise sufficient money for demonstrating conservation efforts. As the effort begins to implement conservation projects, participants noted that funding may come from industry, federal programs, or the conservation credit trading system. Funding for the demonstration projects will potentially be provided by a mix of the partners, including the federal agencies and oil and gas companies.

Provide Incentives

According to the group, the Initiative's partnership is built upon using incentives for landowners, local communities, and private industry to invest in habitat restoration and other conservation actions. The incentives working group has focused its efforts primarily on two incentives. First, the Initiative views the creation of a conservation credit trading system as a potentially significant economic incentive for landowners to engage in voluntary conservation efforts. This system would allow landowners or others to earn credits by implementing sagebrush conservation activities. These credits could then be sold to energy companies or others who may desire them for a variety of purposes, including mitigating the effect of development projects elsewhere in sagebrush habitat. The concepts behind the conservation credit trading system are currently in development and many of the participants acknowledge that there are significant inherent difficulties in designing such a system, particularly one that will stand up to scientific scrutiny. For example, the sagebrush ecosystem is highly heterogeneous, with varying levels of habitat quality across the range. This creates challenges in determining the value of a credit and how this may change from location to location. However, several of the participants we spoke with believed this credit trading system was crucial to the overall Initiative and remained optimistic that it could succeed.

The second type of incentive that the Initiative is working on includes obtaining various assurances from the Department of the Interior that by implementing voluntary sagebrush ecosystem conservation efforts, participants would not bear greater costs or requirements if the greater sage grouse or other species dependent on the sagebrush ecosystem became listed under the Endangered Species Act. For example, if a rancher improved or created habitat for sage grouse on his or her land and then the species was listed under the Endangered Species Act, the rancher could be subject to restrictions on grazing practices that might harm the sage grouse by damaging its habitat. The Initiative developed and submitted five specific recommendations that they believe Interior could take to secure particular assurances. According to one partner, Interior has indicated that the group will receive a response soon.

Monitor Results for Accountability

The group has not yet initiated any conservation projects; however, the group issued a request for proposal in May 2007 for demonstration projects designed to measurably improve sagebrush habitat and test the concept of a conservation credit trading system. The request for proposal included provisions for monitoring of projects. Some participants noted that monitoring would be a critical component of any conservation projects and conservation credit system.

EASTERN UPPER PENINSULA PARTNERS IN ECOSYSTEM MANAGEMENT

The Eastern Upper Peninsula Partners in Ecosystem Management group was started in 1992 originally to collaborate across boundaries on lands in the eastern Upper Peninsula of Michigan for ecosystem management. Over time, the group evolved into an information-sharing group to coordinate land management, but has been relatively inactive in recent years. Members of the group include state and federal government agencies, a conservation organization, and industrial (timber) landowners who together manage two-thirds of the four million acres of the eastern Upper Peninsula. This area includes the 895,000-acre Hiawatha National Forest, 95,000-acre Seney National Wildlife Refuge, 73,000-acre Pictured Rocks National Lakeshore, state land, and privately owned land.

Historically, much of the eastern Upper Peninsula was managed for timber harvest and most of the region was cut by the early 1900s. In the 1800s, loggers harvested pine and shifted to hardwoods in the 1900s as pine trees were cut over. The eastern Upper Peninsula is once again largely forested with second-growth forests including aspen, white birch, and jack pine. In recent years, many of the timber companies have been selling their lands.

Natural Resource Problems

According to group members, there are few contentious issues causing conflict among land managers and owners in the eastern Upper Peninsula, but the group saw an opportunity among the large landowners to cooperate in a manner that could enhance ecosystems across the landscape. Many members note that the primary outcomes of the group have been educating partners with information that they can use in their management, sharing information among the partners, and building relationships. Some of the particular examples of the Eastern Upper Peninsula group's coordinated efforts include the following:

- Most of the eastern Upper Peninsula is second-growth forest, with trees of similar age. Some members of the group sought to establish a mix of trees of different age classes across the landscape to provide healthy habitat for species, in particular, neotropical bird species such as the golden-winged warbler, that use the forests. However, the forest companies that owned land in the eastern Upper Peninsula were focused on commodity production rather than habitat health. The Eastern Upper Peninsula group provided opportunities to educate the industrial landowners that accommodating neotropical birds on their land could be done without affecting their financial bottom line. By coordinating with neighboring landowners to obtain a mix of vegetation over a larger area, the need for any one landowner to achieve all habitat objectives on his or her land alone was reduced.
- To support efforts to manage their land in a complementary manner, members of the group recognized the need for broad-scale mapping that could be used in looking at the overall landscape. As a result, the group coordinated to map and categorize land units in the region into areas with similar physical and biological characteristics, called land type associations. The land type associations have been used to varying extent by the partners as a planning tool and for some

decision making. The group was able to reach consensus on the descriptions of the land classifications, but was unable to agree on the management implications of the ecological descriptions such as the need to use fire to attain a particular age variation in the trees. The partners were concerned that documenting management implications would constrain the activities they could conduct on their land.

Many of the Eastern Upper Peninsula group partners have worked together on individual efforts to enhance their positive effects on the landscape, discuss compatible management, or preserve land. Examples of such efforts include the following:

- Through the relationship built with the Eastern Upper Peninsula group, The Nature Conservancy and a timber company were able to reach agreement on access and save a wetland area from being built over by a road. The timber company wanted to gain access across a nature preserve owned by The Nature Conservancy. The Nature Conservancy originally denied access and the timber company threatened to build a road across a wetland on its land. Through the relationship developed through the Eastern Upper Peninsula group, these organizations were able to discuss the issue and The Nature Conservancy agreed to allow access across its land.
- A National Park Service official noted that the Eastern Upper Peninsula group helped the National Park Service open a dialogue with the state and timber companies to discuss forest management issues. Pictured Rocks National Lakeshore has a 39,300-acre buffer zone of land within its boundary that is predominately owned by the state and timber companies. According to a former National Park Service official, the National Park Service has an interest in maintaining healthy ecosystems in this buffer zone, while the state and timber company's interest is focused primarily on the use of the land to generate revenue from harvesting timber.
- As a result of the relationship that The Nature Conservancy developed with state and federal agencies and timber companies, The Nature Conservancy negotiated a conservation easement on 250,000 acres of private timberland. The easement will allow some forestry on the land, but in a manner that is compatible with a nearby Nature Conservancy preserve.

Collaborative Practices

The collaborative practices used by the Eastern Upper Peninsula group are described in the following sections.

Seek Inclusive Representation

The Eastern Upper Peninsula group effort began when staff from the Michigan Department of Natural Resources recognized the need to talk with the landowners who shared their boundaries and subsequently convened a meeting with the Forest Service, National Park Service, U.S. Fish and Wildlife Service, and The Nature Conservancy. According to these partners, after they had been meeting for a period of time, they recognized the influence of private forest land in the eastern Upper Peninsula landscape. The group members debated about whether or not to bring private timber companies who owned or managed land into the partnership because they were commodity-based and would have different goals and objectives for the land than the agencies. Ultimately, according to the members, they decided to invite timber representatives into the group. One timber industry official noted that his company was initially interested in the Eastern Upper Peninsula group because participating in a collaborative group could help them attain certification for sustainable forestry practices. More recently, the timber companies have had less interest in the group, in part because many of them have been selling their land in the eastern Upper Peninsula.

Develop a Collaborative Process

The participants stressed that the Eastern Upper Peninsula group is not a decision-making group and therefore does not have an established decision-making process. However, the group has used consensus to identify issues that it would like to work on. The group has no protocols, bylaws, or memorandums of understanding. The members share information and, as partners see the need, form subgroups to work on particular projects, with people joining in as they have the interest and time. Under this arrangement, each entity retains its own individual objectives and decision-making process that it will go through to determine what work it will undertake as a part of the group's efforts. Some members noted that the informality of the group has allowed them to avoid issues with the Federal Advisory Committee Act, which establishes rules for federal advisory committees.[7]

Pursue Flexibility, Openness, and Respect

According to the Eastern Upper Peninsula group partners, the participants generated trust because early in the process they agreed to respect the missions of each of the individual organizations and to not change any agency's or organization's mission or objectives. Participants describe trust as the most significant outcome of their efforts. When the group first began meeting, each of the partners discussed their organization's missions, which helped the group to gain an understanding of one another. As a result of the trust generated by the group, they have been able to openly share information that they probably would have not shared otherwise, such as the location of timber harvests. Some participants noted that through the open atmosphere generated by the group, potential conflicts are often eliminated before they become conflicts.

Find Leadership

According to some of the members, the group was pulled together by a few key people who were all managers and able to make decisions. Everyone in the initial group was a manager and had good decision-making skills, an ability to voice his or her opinion, and knowledge of the relevant governing laws, authorities, and policies. Some members noted that different people emerged at various times to bring the group together on different issues and move the group forward.

One of the original members coordinated the group and kept it going between 1992 and 2006. When this person assumed a different position within his agency and was no longer able to coordinate the group, it became less active and does not currently have a coordinator. Some members noted that there were still natural resource issues, such as invasive species, that the group could continue to work on and that the Eastern Upper Peninsula group effort could be improved by having a leader dedicated to the group who had coordination and facilitation skills.

The Natural Resources Conservation Service has not previously been actively involved in the Eastern Upper Peninsula group, according to an official from the agency, but coordinates the Upper Peninsula Resource Conservation and Development Council—a congressionally designated, nonprofit group that identifies and undertakes resource management and community development projects. Some of the council's goals overlap with those of the Eastern Upper Peninsula group. Consequently, the council coordinator, who is a Natural Resources Conservation Service employee, has offered to facilitate and coordinate the group's meetings in the future, starting in early 2008. A Natural Resources Conservation Service official noted that this may supply the impetus needed to get the Eastern Upper Peninsula group active again and working on issues important to the group members.

Identify a Common Goal

The Eastern Upper Peninsula group members agreed that their goal is "to facilitate complementary management of public and private lands, for all appropriate land uses, using a landscape-ecological approach to sustain and enhance representative ecosystems in the Eastern Upper Peninsula of Michigan." According to one of the group's founders, the Eastern Upper Peninsula effort was originally envisioned as a means to coordinate land management strategies and activities among neighboring landowners to achieve overall ecosystem goals. However, after the group began meeting, it became apparent that it would not be able to concur on a common management approach given the different missions of each of the partners. Efforts by some of the members to try to get the partners to coordinate and agree on common management practices and strategies were met with resistance. Consequently, the group determined that it would function as an information-sharing group and not a decision-making body.

Develop a Process for Obtaining Information

The Eastern Upper Peninsula group has placed a high priority on developing and sharing information. The group has worked together to map and describe land type associations in the eastern Upper Peninsula, which some members noted have been useful in making landscape-scale decisions. Members of the group stated that any information developed by the group is made available to other members without restrictions or protocols. For example, land type associations were developed for private lands adjacent to the national forest and were used by small foresters to help with their planning.

Leverage Available Resources

The Eastern Upper Peninsula group has not officially sought funding because, according to group members, it made a decision that it did not want to receive and mange funds. Resources for the group came from the individual partners as they were needed and available. For example, some of the timber company partners published a guide on threatened and endangered species using private funds.

Provide Incentives

The Eastern Upper Peninsula group does not use any particular incentives to achieve its goals.

Monitor Results for Accountability

The Eastern Upper Peninsula group has not established any formal mechanisms to monitor natural resources, but has periodically assessed the need for the group to continue. According to one member, monitoring natural resource improvements made by a group is possible only if the group has joint projects, which is not the case of this group. Furthermore, the group has no resources to dedicate to monitoring. However, group members noted that they assessed the value of the group every 2 or 3 years by evaluating their progress toward their goals and discussing among the members whether the effort was still needed. In addition, every 2 to 3 years the group would discuss and set new goals.

MALPAI BORDERLANDS GROUP

The Malpai Borderlands Group is a nonprofit group in southeastern Arizona and southwestern New Mexico working to restore fire as an ecological process to the rangelands and keep a working landscape based on natural resources—primarily, livestock grazing. The Sonoran and Chihauhaun deserts in this area have historically supported ranching, but also support numerous species, including threatened and endangered species such as the New Mexico ridge-nosed rattlesnake, jaguar, and Chiricauhua leopard frog.

The group's planning and activities encompass approximately 800,000 acres including public lands managed by the Forest Service, BLM, and the states of New Mexico and Arizona, as well as private lands held by ranchers and the nonprofit Animas Foundation. The group started informally, meeting to discuss problems the neighbors faced in ranching and eventually bringing in interested environmentalists who were concerned about subdivision and development of the land, including The Nature Conservancy. The group incorporated in 1994 to more actively pursue its goals.

Natural Resource Problems

In working to restore fire to the landscape, the Malpai group has worked to resolve related problems.

- Wildland fires can provide some beneficial effects to ecosystems that are adapted to fire, such as restoring vegetation and improving habitat. Some landowners view fire as beneficial but others do not want to use fire to manage land and vegetation. For example, Arizona state trust lands are managed primarily for ranching and to generate income for public schools in the state. As a result, the state puts out all fires on these lands and generally does not use fire as a management tool to promote growth of grasses and fuel reduction of shrubs and bushes, although it works with the Malpai Borderland Group to set prescribed fires. On the other hand, the Forest Service, BLM, and some private ranchers want to burn their grasslands to reduce shrubs, such as creosote and mesquite and to promote grasses. The group has worked to educate landowners about the benefits of fire and has worked with the different landowners to set and burn several large fires. The group has succeeded in reintroducing fire to a total of about 69,000 acres.
- The effects of fire on threatened and endangered species are mixed and create difficulties for using fire to restore vegetation. While restoring fire to an ecosystem that is fire-adapted helps support habitats and species in the long term, using fire on the landscape in the short term can harm threatened and endangered species, such as the ridge-nosed rattlesnake, or food sources for other threatened and endangered species, such as the agave plant used by lesser long-nosed bats. The group worked to get the most recent scientific evidence from researchers working on the species to use in their plans to restore fire, both on public and private lands. More recently, the group has begun working on a habitat conservation plan with the U.S. Fish and Wildlife Service, which would identify the activities that could be undertaken by the group without triggering concerns about "taking"—killing or harming—a threatened or endangered species.
- Resource overuse can occur during drought. During an extended drought over the last decade, ranchers in the Malpai area faced a decision to sell off their herds or keep them on the land and potentially overgraze it. To avoid this outcome, the group and the Animas Foundation—a nonprofit working ranch operating within the group's boundaries—established a grassbank on Animas Foundation lands in New Mexico. Ranchers with distressed lands

have used the grassbank for 3 to 5 years. Continued drought has made this program less viable in the last few years as the drought has extended over a broader area.

- Development of open land and loss of the resource and open space occurs when ranchers sell their lands. Private landowners can sell their land at any time, but are more likely to sell during economic hardship. Yet ranchers, and others, have an interest in maintaining open lands for different purposes—livestock grazing, habitat for species, and amenities such as recreation or scenic views. The group worked with ranchers in the area who did not want to sell, purchasing conservation easements for their lands that allowed them to stay in ranching despite economic need to sell the land. The group has succeeded in protecting 77,000 acres of land using conservation easements.
- The group worked with an individual rancher who provided habitat for a threatened species—the Chiricahua leopard frog. As a result, the U.S. Fish and Wildlife Service provided the Malpai Borderlands Group with a safe harbor agreement that protects the owner, and any other landowners who wish to participate, should the species be damaged by typical ranching actions.

Collaborative Practices

The collaborative practices used by the Malpai Borderlands Group are described in the following sections.

Seek Inclusive Representation

The Malpai Borderlands Group began informally as a discussion group that later incorporated as a nonprofit. The original members of the group were self-selected members of the ranching community and interested environmentalists who were associated with members of the group. When the Malpai Borderlands Group incorporated in 1994, this discussion group formed the original board. Many of the members of the Malpai group are landowners in the area, but some are not. The board includes a member of The Nature Conservancy and retired federal employees who were key in helping the group get started and work with the agencies. Board meetings are open and the group invites a wide range of people to attend. It also works with its critics on various issues; however, it has determined not to change the membership of the board to include outside parties because of concerns over control of members' private lands. The members of the group are particularly concerned about the need to recruit young people to the group and board—some are leaving ranching altogether and those who remain often do not attend meetings.

Develop a Collaborative Process

The group is managed by a nonprofit board, which has bylaws and organizational structure. According to some members, the group has succeeded because it is run by the board, and while the agencies have joined the effort, they do not direct it. This is important because the private landowners make decisions about what actions to take on their own lands.

The group coordinates closely with federal and state agencies that manage lands within the Malpai planning area. Until the last few years, two of these agencies—the Natural Resources Conservation Service and the Forest Service—dedicated an employee to be a liaison with the group. When the Natural Resources Conservation Service liaison retired, a new person was selected with the help of the group; however, when the Forest Service liaison retired, the agency and the group decided not to fill that position and the agency is instead trying to have more employees work with the group.

Pursue Flexibility, Openness, and Respect

The group holds open meetings and invites a wide range of participants to talk about management issues. It works by consensus, trying to work problems out informally first. For example, in the mid-1990s, a member of the group photographed a live jaguar in the United States. Members participated in the discussions over protection of the species and designation of critical habitat—specific areas that may be critical for the conservation of the species—for it in the United States. The group invited a key scientist to visit and assess the habitat, and as a result, members believe that what they are doing to restore the habitat and keep it open is the best protection for the habitat. The Malpai group also established a fund to reimburse ranchers for any jaguar kills of livestock. While members of the group disagree with the need for the federal government to designate critical habitat for the species in the United States, which may have an effect on the activities that they can conduct on their land, they invited environmental groups to their board meetings to discuss protection of the species under the Endangered Species Act. According to the Center for Biological Diversity, a member attended a meeting but the groups disagreed on how to handle the situation. The U.S. Fish and Wildlife Service listed the jaguar as endangered outside of the United States in 1972, prohibiting the import of jaguar pelts into the country, and listed it as endangered within the United States under the Endangered Species Act in 1997. Recently, the Center has sued the U.S. Fish and

Wildlife Service to compel the agency to develop a recovery plan and designate critical habitat for the jaguar.

Find Leadership

Members of the Malpai group attribute their success to the leadership of several individuals who brought vision, commitment, and organizational skills to the group. They also recognized the role played by federal agency officials both in Washington and in the field offices, who recognized the group's potential and gave it the opportunity—and resources, including people—to work. According to members, leadership and organizational skills from The Nature Conservancy were also key to getting foundations interested in the group's efforts and getting the group incorporated as a nonprofit. Most importantly, key members of the ranching community had the vision to join together—when most ranchers prefer to work as individuals—and other farsighted ranchers joined them. Members attribute this attitude to a particular individual whose philosophy was to protect the land and those who work it.

Identify a Common Goal

The Malpai group's goal is to "restore and maintain the natural processes that create and protect healthy, unfragmented landscape to support a diverse, flourishing community of human, plant, and animal life in our borderlands region. Together, we will accomplish this by working to encourage profitable ranching and other traditional livelihoods which will sustain the open space nature of our land for generations to come." When lands in the area started selling, these ranchers became concerned about future subdivision and development of ranchland and the potential loss of their ranching livelihoods and joined together to protect both. Another concern was the lack of fire.

Develop a Process for Obtaining Information

As part of its decision-making process, the Malpai Borderland Group seeks to gather and use scientific information relevant to the problem its members are managing. The group has a science coordinator whose position is to manage several ongoing research efforts on lands in the Malpai planning area and a Science Advisory Board made up of more than 40 experts in rangeland science; this group provides advice about research efforts, monitoring, and management activities. These include a program of research to study the effects of wildland fire on threatened and endangered species such as the lesser long-nosed bat and ridge-nosed rattlesnake. The science program also includes 9,000 acres of research plots established by the Forest Service's Rocky Mountain Research Station to study different revegetation treatments in areas excluded from grazing and 12 watersheds to examine the sediment runoff resulting from burning differently-sized areas and different amounts of vegetation. The group funds research, as well as partners with outside researchers from federal agencies, such as USDA's research stations, and universities. In addition, the group sponsors an annual scientific conference on topics related to its interests and management activities.

Leverage Available Resources

Because the group fosters a cooperative relationship among landowners and agency staff to manage a broad landscape, it has been able to raise more money for its conservation efforts. Private fundraising groups and individuals provide funding to groups that can achieve on-the-ground resource improvements and results. The group received start-up funds, which was important because it let the group buy basic office equipment such as computers, printers, and supplies. Over the years, the group has met at one of the ranch houses, in an addition built for the meetings. The group continues to get grants from nonprofit groups such as the National Fish and Wildlife Foundation and receives grants for research and personnel support.

Most of the members have been involved since the inception of the discussion group and acknowledge the heavy time commitment that comes with being part of the group. The members see the benefit of participating because as a group they are able to accomplish activities that they would not do as individuals. For example, prior to the establishment of the group, one rancher could not coordinate with the agencies to burn vegetation on both his land and on the agency's adjacent land. The group used to meet monthly, but now meets less often. Because the distances between ranches are great and require considerable travel time, the group conducts business by telephone conference and e-mail and holds quarterly board meetings in person.

Provide Incentives

Incentives used by the group include a grassbank, which allows ranchers to temporarily move their cattle from their own drought-damaged land to healthier grasslands on the Gray Ranch owned by the Animas Foundation. In exchange, the Malpai Borderlands Group receives a conservation easement for the development rights to the private property on the ranch. These conservation easements are different from others used by The Nature Conservancy and federal agencies in that they contain a clause that states if the rancher loses access to his or her federal grazing allotment through no fault of his or her own, then the easement is void and the land could then be sold for development.

The group has worked with U.S. Fish and Wildlife Service to manage the threatened and endangered species on privately-owned ranchlands in the group's planning area. In one case, the group received a safe harbor agreement to protect one of the last remaining populations of Chiricahua leopard frogs that were residing in a rancher's stock pond. The agreement allows the rancher, who had trucked water in to the pond during drought years to keep the frogs alive, to manage the stock pond for livestock purposes without the threat of enforcement action should any of the frogs die because of those actions. Other ranchers can participate in the safe harbor agreement by signing a certificate of inclusion with the Malpai Borderlands Group and thereby receive the protections of the agreement. The group is also developing a habitat conservation plan for the area in order to implement grassland and ranch management activities in areas where there are threatened or endangered species. For example, this habitat conservation plan will allow the use of fire in certain conditions and identify certain restrictions to protect the threatened ridge-nosed rattlesnake and several other species that might be harmed or killed by the fires. This will permit ranchers to conduct activities provided the restrictions are followed.

Monitor Results for Accountability

As part of its management efforts, the group conducts range monitoring across the lands in its planning area and maintains more than 290 monitoring plots for this purpose. It pays a contractor to visit the plots to determine the condition of the pastures and the availability and use of grass by livestock or wildlife. According to members, these monitoring efforts are useful for judging the condition of grasslands in the vicinity of the plots, but do not gauge overall rangeland conditions. The group is working on a method for monitoring range conditions more broadly across the whole planning area. The group has also sponsored species counts for some of the threatened and endangered species on lands in its planning area. This work enabled them to better know and understand the location of species and to limit activities there.

Onslow Bight Conservation Forum

The Onslow Bight Conservation Forum (Forum)—named for the shallow crescent-shaped bay that makes up much of the coastline in southeastern North Carolina where the group is organized—is an information-sharing group organized to help protect and restore the unique coastal environment of the area and associated species. The Onslow Bight region, as with other parts of coastal North Carolina, is developing quickly and the rural nature of the area is rapidly changing. Because of its unique makeup, the area is a hotspot for endemic species—those that can only be found in that area—such as the Venus flytrap. This area of North Carolina contains both longleaf pine habitat favored by the endangered red-cockaded woodpecker and unique wetland habitat such as pocosins, or wetlands that form on a hill because of large amounts of peat that accumulate.

The group, formed officially in 2001, originally began as a way to help the Marine Corps manage encroachment issues around its installations and to manage habitat for threatened and endangered species, in particular the red-cockaded woodpecker. The group has since expanded its vision to include aquatic habitat and conservation of land along the coast. The members of the group represent the large blocks of publicly-owned lands such as the North Carolina Wildlife Resources Commission game lands, the Croatan National Forest, Marine Corps Base Camp Lejune, Marine Corps Air Station Cherry Point, and several land conservation trust groups. In addition to overall biodiversity conservation, one focus of the group has been to study potential corridors for wildlife to migrate between these public lands.

Natural Resource Problems

The natural resource management problems and conflicts that the Forum has managed revolve around land development and conservation:

- Development of lands eliminates habitat for different species and causes the public lands to become islands of biodiversity, which can affect management of these lands. In particular, development can harm endangered species such as the red-cockaded woodpecker. Agencies with populations that need to be protected are interested in expanding habitat to help protect the species and ease the pressure on their lands. Yet, private landowners are free to sell and develop their land. The Forum developed a habitat protection plan to identify the location of important habitat for threatened and endangered species and has discussed and agreed upon areas that are a priority for preservation and protection. This information has helped the agencies and land trusts coordinate and prioritize land acquisition and has prevented them from competing for the same lands. Since 2001, the Forum partners have together acquired about 57,000 acres of land from willing sellers.

- Encroachment near military installations creates safety hazards as well as complaints from neighboring communities about noise, dust, and other side-effects of training exercises. The military has the incentive to use its lands for training purposes and to have large buffers between its installations and communities. Yet, communities and others have incentives to develop lands for other purposes. Through the Forum, the Marine Corps representatives can work with other members to identify lands that have compatible uses with the military's needs and also meet habitat purposes. Military funds can then be used to help acquire conservation easements to the land.
- Habitat fragmentation occurs with increased development, particularly with greater numbers and size of roads, which affects large species and increases vehicle collisions with wildlife that are possibly fatal. Private landowners have the right to sell and develop their land and zoning allows for building. However, hunting, environmental, and other groups have an interest in protecting species such as the black bear, which need land to roam. The Onslow Bight area supports a large population of bears and the number of collisions with wildlife in the area is increasing. The group has identified areas that road construction should avoid and the need for more wildlife crossings in new road construction.
- Historically, the longleaf pine and pocosins of the Coastal Plain depended on fire as an ecological process. Fire has been suppressed for years, although the health of the vegetation depends on fire. The agencies and land managers have an interest in burning their lands to restore their health, however, new community members do not like smoke and complain about burning programs. The group is working with The Nature Conservancy on a project started in 2005 called the Onslow Bight Fire Learning Network/LANDFIRE application project to develop and support a burn program to help restore habitat.[8] The Nature Conservancy is also developing a memorandum of understanding (MOU) with the Forum to share equipment and personnel. Including burning on agency lands as part of the fire programs, the members of the Forum burn about 60,000 acres of land a year.

Collaborative Practices

The collaborative practices used by the Forum are described in the following sections.

Seek Inclusive Representation

The Forum includes a range of participants who manage land or are advocates for land conservation. The Forum began with a network of land managers and federal and state agency officials, and members have discussed how broadly to advertise for potential members; for now, they have determined to keep the membership more narrow. Two land conservation organizations—North Carolina Coastal Federation and North Carolina Coastal Land Trust—have representatives in the Forum. Members also include representatives from the North Carolina Natural Heritage Program, which conducts inventories for rare species and high-quality habitat in the state, and the Wildlife Resources Commission, which manages state lands for wildlife. Another state agency, the Department of Transportation, has signed on as a member because it acquires lands to mitigate the destruction of wetlands or other lands for road building activities. It is also interested in identifying where to put underpasses for wildlife to safely cross roads; however, members indicated that agency representation has been infrequent.

In addition to the Marine Corps, other federal agencies that are involved in the Forum include the Forest Service, U.S. Fish and Wildlife Service, and the National Park Service. The federal partners were initially more involved in planning efforts, but because the key staff involved left the area and were not replaced, the agencies have had less involvement. Members of the U.S. Fish and Wildlife Service Ecological Services group participate because of threatened and endangered species issues. Other federal employees from the Forest Service have attended as they are able to do so, but according to Forum and Forest Service members, other Forest Service activities compete for their attention. The Natural Resources Conservation Service also joined the Forum and attends meetings. However, while Forum members see a role for the agency because of the large amounts of conservation funding that it provides, the agency has been less involved in acquisition activities because that is not a main goal of the Natural Resources Conservation Service.

Develop a Collaborative Process

The Forum exists through an MOU signed by all members. The MOU is nonbinding and states that each agency will retain its mission. It also states that the group will discuss and share information that is compatible with the land use and management objectives of each entity involved. The MOU allows the groups to discuss, share information, and agree on conservation or preservation opportunities, but in order to avoid triggering Federal Advisory Committee Act requirements, the group does not make official decisions or take official actions. For committees subject to the Federal Advisory Committee Act, the act generally requires that agencies announce committee meetings ahead of time and give notice to interested parties about such meetings. With some exceptions, the meetings are to be open to the public, and agencies are to prepare meeting minutes and make them available to interested parties. Nevertheless, the Forum can come to consensus on activities, which individual agencies can decide to undertake or not.

Pursue Flexibility, Openness, and Respect

According to members, because of the MOU, which allows each member to retain its overall mission and undertake the activities that best suit that mission, the group is highly flexible and open. In addition, participants said that the Forum has been managed in a transparent manner, in that the participants are clear in sharing their individual interests with other members. Participants said that this transparency has helped to foster respect among the members. For example, the Marine Corps members have been upfront about their purpose in working for land conservation, which involves relieving the pressure of development around their installations and potentially removing restrictions on training exercises that result from threatened and endangered species habitat.

Find Leadership

The Forum started with the efforts of two key people with The Nature Conservancy and the U.S. Marine Corps, modeled after a similar effort at the Army's Fort Bragg in North Carolina. It has continued with the sustained interest of several more individuals. Members participate as they are able and as they can offer particular skills. Because these individuals and their agencies have sustained the Forum by such efforts as organizing meetings and completing work between meetings, the group is currently discussing whether it should hire staff to ensure that work gets accomplished. The participants are uncertain which of the agencies or groups could justify funding such a position and to whom that position would answer.

Identify a Common Goal

The goal of the Forum is to provide for open discussion about the long-term conservation and enhancement of biological diversity and ecosystem sustainability in the Onslow Bight area. The members have different goals for managing their land and resources, but do share the goal of identifying opportunities to preserve, protect, and restore native biological elements in the coastal landscape, including marine and estuarine areas. To achieve their goal, the group has focused on acquiring lands that bridge the gaps between large publicly-owned lands, as well as some private conservation lands, and can meet their common needs. For example, one species on which the group focuses is the red-cockaded woodpecker; two of the federal partners have primary habitat for this species and support two of the main recovery populations of the bird as defined by the U.S. Fish and Wildlife Service in its recovery plan for the species. The group has identified, and has acquired, land between the public lands that can serve as a stepping-stone for members of the populations. The group recognizes that acquisition is only the first step of protecting land and resources. The next step is to restore habitat and manage those acquired lands and resources in the long term. Most of the land is being managed by the state's Department of Environment and Natural Resources, primarily the Wildlife Resources Commission and the Division of Parks and Recreation.

Develop a Process for Obtaining Information

In developing its habitat protection plan, the Forum made use of available information about lands and resources in the area. In particular, the state's Natural Heritage Program conducts assessments of habitat and identifies good habitat for purposes of preserving and protecting it, and the Forum used this data to develop the plan. It also used information on existing populations of species such as bears and red-cockaded woodpeckers and locations of undeveloped woodlands. The Forum also used the scientific expertise available from the federal and state agencies in its planning process. Biologists from the federal and state agencies helped to identify how species such as bears and woodpeckers move across the landscape and, accordingly, good places to protect.

Leverage Available Resources

Members of the Forum have been successful in getting grants and using these funds to match agency funding to acquire lands. According to participants, one of the benefits of the Forum is that foundations and other funding groups use collaboration as a way to judge the potential success and effectiveness of the group. Sources of funding include the military, North Carolina trust funds established for purposes of land conservation, U.S. Fish and Wildlife Service grants under the North American Wetland Conservation Act, and funds raised by the land conservation group partners. The Forest Service also attempted to get funding from the Land and Water Conservation Fund, but did not succeed.

The Forum does not have staff and its work is done by the participants, which means that sometimes it does not get done. The group meets every few months and keeps in touch by e-mail, but participants may not be able to prioritize or complete tasks for the group in between meetings. The Forum discussed hiring staff but has not made a decision to do so. According to members, having staff would allow the group to get more work done in between meetings and would ensure that the work would be done. The decision to have staff is difficult, however, because the action might force the group members to increase their commitment to the group through funding the position or even cause the Forum to take on a different organizational structure to enable the hiring of staff.

Provide Incentives

Apart from the incentives provided by land acquisition, the group has not had the opportunity to provide or use any incentives to achieve its goals. However, in the future, the group may need to work more with private landowners and provide them incentives. Some members cited Natural Resources Conservation Service programs to protect and conserve agricultural lands and wetlands as potential sources of funding to work with landowners. For example, one program that could potentially be compatible with the Forum's goals is the Wetlands Reserve Program, a program that seeks to restore marginal agricultural land to its previous wetland condition through cost-share assistance and easement purchases. According to the agency's Forum representative, the agency's staff currently works with landowners on more traditional agricultural issues such as preventing erosion and conserving soils.

Monitor Results for Accountability

As membership in the Forum is voluntary, any activities the participants undertake are also voluntary and the Forum does not track its achievements. These activities, primarily land acquisition and some restoration work, help the Forum achieve its overall vision of protecting habitat. This conclusion is based on the assumption that protecting and restoring habitat will improve species conditions. As part of its planning effort, the Forum has developed a geographic information system (GIS) map of the public lands and locations of important species and habitat. Because the lands are acquired by each agency or participant and not by the Forum, this map is not updated to show acquisitions or to keep track of the lands protected. Rather, the information that the group develops about habitat and species can be used by each participant as it makes decisions about land acquisition.

Steens Mountain Advisory Council

The Steens Mountain Cooperative Management and Protection Area (CMPA), located in southeastern Oregon, was created in 2000 when Congress passed the Steens Mountain Cooperative Management and Protection Act (Steens Act).[9] The high desert mountain area occupies about 496,000 acres and supports diverse vegetation and wildlife, including habitat for the sage grouse. The same area has a long history of human use as a Native American site for spiritual experience and herbal gathering and for cattle grazing by local ranching families. The purpose of the CMPA is for BLM "to conserve, protect, and manage the long-term ecological integrity of Steens Mountain for future and present generations." Of the 496,000 acres in the CMPA, about 428,000 acres are federal lands and the remaining lands are private and state lands. The Steens Act protected about 170,000 acres of the federally managed land as wilderness, of which about 95,000 acres are specifically designated as a cattle-free wilderness, the first of its kind.[10] The federal land is managed for various uses by BLM, and BLM is authorized to work cooperatively with private land owners in managing the entire area.

Natural Resource Problems

The Steens Act established a multistakeholder group called the Steens Mountain Advisory Council (Council). The Council is charged with providing BLM recommendations regarding "new and unique approaches to the management of lands within the boundaries of the CMPA and cooperative programs and incentives for seamless landscape management that meets human needs and maintains and improves the ecological and economic integrity of the CMPA." The major land and resource management issues that the Council has considered are described below:

- The act required that BLM develop a comprehensive management plan for the Steens Mountain CMPA. In addition to the wilderness area created by the act, the CMPA contains several wilderness study areas that BLM must manage to retain wilderness conditions and wild and scenic river corridors that BLM must manage to maintain natural conditions. These designations may limit certain activities, such as motorized vehicles and equipment, in the areas, and as a result, Council members disagree over how to manage these areas—ranchers and others would like the wilderness study areas to be removed from consideration as wilderness, but an environmental group would like even more area to be considered as wilderness study area. In August 2005, BLM, with the Council's input, issued a land management plan; however, it did not completely address management of roads and travel in the CMPA, deferring decisions on route designations until 2007.

- Travel management and designation of roads, tire tracks, and ways for traditional access was an issue discussed in 2007. BLM has been charged with managing travel in the CMPA and can potentially restrict travel in some places, in particular the new wilderness area and other wilderness study areas. Although motorized access to wilderness areas and wilderness study areas is limited, participants of the Council have not been able to agree on the definitions for different types of roads that should remain open for access. Given the historic uses of Steens Mountain, the area has many roads, tracks, or ways that are used at various times and for multiple reasons—such as to access property each day, check on fencing periodically, and gather herbs during different seasons. However, some of these have been proposed for closure by environmental groups in order to maintain wilderness characteristics of the wilderness areas and study areas, as required by law. An initial travel management plan was made public in May 2007, but was rescinded due to a court order and was reissued in November 2007.
- Private land management within the CMPA is another management issue in which the Council has been involved. BLM is authorized to work with private landowners within the CMPA to cooperatively manage the private and public lands, such as to control vegetation. However, BLM has been able to agree in only a few cases on what management activities and payments will be involved. At least one owner is considering selling his land for development rather than working with BLM. The act authorizes $25 million from the land and water conservation fund for, among other purposes, the acquisition of private land and conservation easements within the CMPA. According to the agency and Council members, none of these funds have been provided, limiting the actions local BLM officials can take. Council members and others explained that by adding new layers of management restrictions, such as wilderness management restrictions, the act limited their ability to manage the area in a new and innovative way, thereby precluding some cooperation and creative management that could have taken place.

One area in which the group has agreed is related to vegetation management. The Council has endorsed a juniper management program to thin stands of juniper that have expanded and overcome sagebrush habitats and grasslands in the area. BLM, with Council input, is studying different options for reducing the expansion of juniper woodlands, but to date only limited activity has been funded. According to the agency, the Council has had greater success at working together to solve ecological restoration issues.

Collaborative Practices

The collaborative practices used by the Council are described in the following sections.

Seek Inclusive Representation

The Council consists of 12 representatives that, according to the Steens Act, must be appointed by the Secretary of the Interior from nominees submitted by various federal, state, and local officials. Members include, among others: a private landowner in the CMPA; two members who are grazing permittees on federal lands in the CMPA; a member interested in fish and recreational fishing in the CMPA; a member of the Burns Paiute Tribe; two persons who are recognized environmental representatives, one of whom represents the state as a whole and one of whom is from the local area; a person who participates in dispersed recreation such as hiking, camping, nature viewing or photography, bird watching, horse back riding, or trail walking; and a person who is a recreational permit holder or is a representative of a commercial recreation operation in the CMPA. Several members noted that the group stalemates as a result of their makeup and difficulty in getting a quorum. According to several members and observers, the group is polarized on fundamental issues of use versus nonuse and some suggested the need for more neutral or balanced representation.

Another community group, similar to the Blackfoot Challenge in Montana and the Malpai Borderlands Group in Arizona and New Mexico, has formed with the help of the staff at the local U.S. Fish and Wildlife Service refuge. This group, called the High Desert Partnership, has succeeded in working together on a few projects and has helped rebuild trust with the U.S. Fish and Wildlife Service among some community members. One difference is that the group is focused on the common interests of the members.

Develop a Collaborative Process

The Council's organization and processes have evolved, although members of the Council and others explained that it has been less successful making recommendations because of organizational problems. Although the Council votes using a majority rule, it was not until March 2006 that members adopted operating protocols that describe, among other things, the Council's objectives, roles and responsibilities, and communication protocols. The Council needs 9 votes in order to provide BLM with a formal recommendation; however, during the several years the group has been in existence, attendance has been poor and filling vacancies has been a problem, making it difficult for it to establish a quorum for votes to take place. According to several members of the Council, they believe they have failed to make recommendations on large issues but they have made decisions about less important issues. More recently, all vacancies have been filled and some participants were more optimistic about the Council's ability to collaborate in the future. In 2007, the Council provided approximately 20 recommendations.

BLM has brought in an outside facilitator to help the Council work through conflicts. The facilitator worked with the members during a 2-day retreat and made progress on a wilderness access issue. However, a later vote by the Council failed to approve the final plan.

Pursue Flexibility, Openness, and Respect

At times, the group has lacked a respectful atmosphere. One observer explained that at one of the Council's meetings some members fostered disrespect toward BLM representatives and tried to direct BLM decisions rather than simply provide advice. In response to such issues, the March 2006 protocols include a section on rules for members and members of the public to follow in order to facilitate an open and collaborative discussion. These rules say that members will listen with respect, avoid grandstanding in order to allow everyone a fair chance to speak and to contribute, and jointly advocate for support for consensus recommendations.

Find Leadership

According to the agency and participants, the group needs a strong leader or facilitator with sufficient training to guide the group. The Council has a regular facilitator from the local area; however, at least one member believes the group requires stronger facilitation to move forward. While the U.S. Institute for Environmental Conflict Resolution provided the Council with third-party facilitation in 2003 that achieved consensus on some travel access issues, the facilitation was short term and the consensus did not last.

Identify a Common Goal

While one objective of the Steens Act was to promote and foster cooperation, communication, and understanding and to reduce conflict between Steens Mountain users and interests, members and other parties said that conflicting interpretations of the act are a fundamental source of conflict among parties. According to several BLM officials, cooperation among stakeholders was much better before the act. The Steens Mountain area has been considered an area worthy of conservation since at least 1999, when the area was considered for designation as a national monument but local stakeholders opposed special designation. For this reason, Council members have fundamentally different interpretations of the act, and continue to debate the conservation versus use clauses in it. Council members interpret the act differently—some refer to one of the statutory objectives of the CMPA that promotes grazing and a provision that allows reasonable access to lands within the CMPA, while others assert that a section requiring BLM to ensure the conservation, protection, and improved ecological integrity of the CMPA represents the act's primary purpose. After the establishment of the CMPA and the wilderness area within it, a local environmental group identified several new possible wilderness areas—called wilderness study areas. The group has since sued BLM to designate these areas as wilderness study areas. In June 2007, the District Court held that BLM had properly declined to adopt most of the group's proposed designations.

Develop a Process for Obtaining Information

The Steens Act authorizes BLM to establish a committee of scientists to provide advice on questions relating to the management of the CMPA, but BLM has not done so. A BLM official said that the reason a scientific group has not been formed is lack of funding requested by the scientists who were invited to participate. The local USDA Agriculture Research Service office has partnered with BLM and several private landowners over the last 30 years on scientific research including juniper management. On other issues, such as travel management, the county pulled together a common database for BLM and the Council to use in its discussions about access.

The Steens Act established a Wildlands Juniper Management Area for experimentation, education, interpretation, and demonstration of management that is intended to restore the historic fire regime and native vegetation communities on Steens Mountain. The area is being used to demonstrate different ways BLM and partners are working to reduce the amount or size of juniper woodlands to effectively manage the expansion of juniper vegetation. Some additional experimentation may occur in the area and in other areas of the CMPA. The results of research can help the agency, with Council input, determine the best way to reduce vegetation using all available tools in many areas, and for certain areas including wilderness and wild rivers, through minimum use of mechanized transport or motorized equipment.

Leverage Available Resources

BLM pays between $70,000 and $80,000 annually for the Council's travel, staff support, and facilitation. Because it is an advisory committee, it is not organized to collect donations or spend funds. However, the Steens Act authorized $25 million to be appropriated to BLM to help purchase private properties within the boundaries of the CMPA, and additional funds would be available for incentive payments for cooperative agreements with private landowners. Several members of the Council and others told us that many conflicts might have been resolved had BLM received these funds.[11] For example, funding could have been used to develop cooperative agreements or purchase private inholdings, thereby reducing controversial issues over access and permissible use.

Provide Incentives

According to the Steens Act, BLM may provide conservation incentive payments[12] to private landowners in the CMPA who enter into a contract with BLM to protect or enhance ecological resources on the private land covered by the contract, if those protections or enhancements benefit public lands. However, according to BLM officials and Council members, because funding has not been forthcoming, such agreements had not been finalized at the time of our review. In 2007, BLM initiated several cooperative management agreements concerning joint juniper management projects where each party pays its own costs and one agreement that provides public recreation on private lands where BLM funds were used (not land and water conservation funds).

Monitor Results for Accountability

The Steens Act requires that a monitoring program be implemented for federal lands in the CMPA so that progress toward ecological integrity objectives can be determined. BLM developed a plan to monitor changes to current resource conditions within the CMPA, which would provide information on 31 resources and uses identified in the CMPA management plan.

The Council has not been formally evaluated to determine its contributions or shortcomings. According to the agency and an observer, the group's effectiveness should be evaluated, particularly because some federal dollars contribute to its functioning.

Uncompahgre Plateau Project

The Uncompahgre Plateau Project is a collaborative group working to restore and sustain the condition of the 1.5-million-acre Uncompahgre Plateau, located in southwestern Colorado. The group began in the late 1990s in response to a decline in the mule deer population on the plateau that was observed by wildlife officials and hunters. After recognizing that the mule deer decline was an indicator of a larger ecosystem problem, the group broadened its focus to restoring and sustaining the ecological, social, cultural, and economic values of the plateau. The group, which includes federal agencies, a community group, a state wildlife agency, and utility companies, has developed a plan, the Uncompahgre Plateau Project Plan, to guide its efforts.

Historically, the Uncompahgre Plateau, 75 percent of which is managed by the BLM, the Forest Service, and the Colorado Division of Wildlife (CDOW), has had multiple uses including logging, ranching, and recreation and provides habitat for many wildlife species, including game species. Commercial logging has occurred on Forest Service land for over a century, but in recent decades the Forest Service has decreased timber harvest on the plateau and current logging operations are limited to small sales of logs and firewood. Both the Forest Service and BLM manage grazing allotments on the plateau that are tied to privately owned ranches. Recreational use of the plateau has steadily increased and includes fishing, off-highway vehicle use, snowmobiling, mountain biking, camping, and cross-country skiing. In addition, CDOW manages two areas on the plateau for deer and elk hunting. Furthermore, the plateau contains lynx analysis units designated by CDOW and the U.S. Fish and Wildlife Service for lynx populations that were reintroduced into Colorado beginning in 1999.

Natural Resource Problems

The Uncompahgre Plateau Project has concentrated on several natural resource problems on the plateau, including the following:

- According to the group's participants, their focus broadened to larger ecosystem health issues when state biologists found that the observed decline in mule deer was related to poor habitat, specifically, vegetation that was too homogeneous in its age class distribution. According to natural resource managers, this condition resulted from certain activities on the plateau such as fire suppression and grazing practices. The Uncompahgre Plateau Project has initiated landscape-level planning and restoration efforts across jurisdictional boundaries to achieve more heterogeneous vegetation across the plateau and bring vegetation structure, age, condition, and spatial patterns in line with the habitat needs of wildlife species. The group's initial planning and restoration efforts have focused on two watersheds covering over 220,000 acres of BLM, Forest Service, state, and private land and has included a variety of vegetation treatments such as roller chopping—using a large round drum to crush the shrubs—and prescribed burning. As of May 2007, the Uncompahgre Plateau Project completed over 100 restoration projects, covering over 50,000 acres.
- The Uncompahgre Plateau has had problems with invasive species on both public and private lands. Invasive species alter the ecology in an area by crowding out native species, changing fire regimes, or altering hydrologic conditions. To facilitate cooperation among land managers and private landowners in efforts to manage invasive species, the Uncompahgre Plateau Project has initiated a program to map, monitor, control, and prevent invasive species within designated weed management areas on over 350,000 acres.
- The Uncompahgre Plateau is a key location for east to west transmission lines connecting Rocky Mountain power sources with western markets such as Los Angeles. As a result of the Energy Policy Act of 2005, transmission line operators must ensure that their power lines remain reliable. Forested rights-of-way pose threats to reliability because of the potential for tall trees to fall on the lines, arcing from the power line to trees, and forest fires. Traditionally, power line rights-of-way have been clear-cut to remove tall trees underneath and adjacent to the power lines, which has historically generated conflict between utilities and land managers, according to a utility official. While this practice removes the threat to power lines directly posed by these trees, it can damage habitat and ecosystem health and the risk from forest

fires still remains. Through the Uncompahgre Plateau Project, the utility companies and land management agencies have worked together to treat vegetation outside of the utility rights-of-way in order to reduce the risk of forest fires and threats to the power lines in a manner that creates more natural openings that are friendly to wildlife. This is accomplished through means such as creating undulating boundaries between treated and untreated vegetation, instead of straight lines. According to a group member, these treatment techniques are being used as a model for other utilities across the country.

- When conducting restoration projects, land managers working on the Uncompahgre Plateau want to replant with vegetation that is native to the plateau because it is better adapted to the local conditions and can improve the success of restoration projects. However, there is not a sufficient supply of native seeds available on the commercial market for large-scale restoration projects on the Uncompahgre Plateau. In response, the Uncompahgre Plateau Project initiated a native plant program to collect, study, and produce native seeds that can be used to facilitate restoration projects. According to a group member, it has gathered native seeds for over 50 plants and developed methods for propagating these. The ultimate goal of this program is to have private, local growers and larger commercial growers cultivate the seeds and sell them to the agencies and energy companies who are doing restoration projects.

Collaborative Practices

The collaborative practices used by the Uncompahgre Plateau Project are described in the following sections.

Seek Inclusive Representation

The Uncompahgre Plateau Project partners include BLM; Forest Service; CDOW; utility companies including the Western Area Power Administration and Tri-State Generation and Transmission Association, Inc.; and an informal nonprofit community organization called the Public Lands Partnership. The Uncompahgre Plateau Project was initiated by the Public Lands Partnership and major land managers on the Uncompahgre Plateau—BLM, Forest Service, and CDOW. Later, the Western Area Power Administration and Tri-State Generation and Transmission Association, Inc., approached the Uncompahgre Plateau Project after seeing a presentation on the group and realizing that working collaboratively to treat vegetation beyond the utility rights-of-way and decrease the threat of forest fires could mutually benefit themselves and the original partners. The Western Area Power Administration and Tri-State Generation and Transmission Association, Inc., became formal partners in the Uncompahgre Plateau Project in 2004.

Many participants cited the involvement of the Public Lands Partnership as a significant and unique asset to the Uncompahgre Plateau Project. The membership of the Public Lands Partnership is made up of county commissioners, city administrators, user groups from the timber industry, agricultural producers, environmentalists, recreationists, and local citizens. The organization started in 1992 because members of the community wanted to get involved in discussions about the public lands that surrounded them. The group brings together members of the public to discuss issues related to public lands including oil and gas drilling, forest plans, campground closures, travel access, and roads. BLM officials noted that, by having the Public Lands Partnership involved in the Uncompahgre Plateau Project, they have been able to complete their National Environmental Policy Act analyses more efficiently because, through the Public Lands Partnership, the public was brought in to help set the vision for the proposed action and there were no subsequent appeals.

Develop a Collaborative Process

The Uncompahgre Plateau Project operates by consensus and, through its efforts, seeks to develop strong communication, collaborative learning, and partnerships among the agencies and community. Individual projects to be undertaken by the group are prioritized by a Technical Committee according to criteria established in the Uncompahgre Plateau Project Plan that was developed by the group. One participant noted that having a collaborative group allows the partners to take a project of theirs and see how it fits into the overall landscape.

The Uncompahgre Plateau Project was formalized with a Cooperative Agreement and MOU, signed in 2001. When that MOU expired at the end of 2006, it was replaced by a second MOU. The structure of the group includes an Executive Committee, Technical Committee, coordinators, and a fiscal agent. The Executive Committee is responsible for annually reviewing project progress and addressing future resource commitments. The Technical Committee forms the working body and backbone of the group and meets monthly to coordinate activities, meet with outside members, review project requests, and recommend budgeting and project approvals. Members from each of the partner organizations hold positions on both the Executive and Technical Committees. In addition to these committees, the Uncompahgre Plateau Project contracted four part-time coordinators who are responsible for public relations and outreach, overall project coordination, financial record keeping and contracting, and grant writing. Some participants noted that the coordinators play a critical role in moving the group forward between meetings and making sure that projects get done. The Uncompahgre Plateau Project uses Uncompahgre/Com, Inc., a nonprofit organization, as its fiscal agent.

Pursue Flexibility, Openness, and Respect

One participant noted that the group was able to generate credibility and trust among the members through the group's initial effort to develop a landscape plan for a watershed around a common vision. According to the participants, the group maintains transparency by having open meetings, distributing minutes of meetings, and using its Web site.

Find Leadership

Several participants attributed the initial success of the group to the leadership of the individual who was originally responsible for coordinating the group. He was described by several participants as a "charismatic leader" who had great vision for the group and was able to get projects going by working with the different agencies to generate support for the collaborative effort.

Identify a Common Goal

While each of the Uncompahgre Plateau Project participants has different interests, they have identified that their common interest is to protect and restore the ecosystem on the Uncompahgre Plateau. The participants were able to agree on a common goal to: "improve the ecosystem health and natural functions of the landscape across the Uncompahgre Plateau through active restoration projects using the best science available and public input," which represents the area where each of the partners' individual interests overlap. The federal land management agencies—BLM and Forest Service—are responsible for managing multiple uses on the plateau, including timber, grazing, and recreation, and have an interest in conducting these management activities in a manner that preserves ecosystem health. CDOW is responsible for managing game species, so it is interested in ensuring that habitat for the mule deer and other game species is healthy and adequate to support them. The Public Lands Partnership represents the community's values and is consequently interested in maintaining a healthy ecosystem for economic, environmental, cultural, social, recreation, and aesthetic reasons. The utility companies desire a healthy ecosystem, less prone to catastrophic wildfires, in order to protect the reliability of their power lines.

Develop a Process for Obtaining Information

According to participants, the Uncompahgre Plateau Project is always seeking new science to inform its decisions and looks for opportunities to bring new ideas to the table. For example, the group works with researchers from universities such as Colorado State University, Brigham Young University, Snow College, and the University of Wyoming to gather new scientific data on the vegetation and ecology of the plateau and study the effects of different vegetation treatments. Scientific publications related to research on the plateau are available on the Uncompahgre Plateau Project Web site. The Uncompahgre Plateau Project frequently sponsors field trips, which one participant noted is important to get community members involved, understand the resource problems that exist on the plateau, and become comfortable with the projects being carried out by the group.

As part of the Uncompahgre Plateau Project planning efforts, BLM and the Forest Service have integrated their GIS map data for two priority watersheds and are working to integrate data for two other priority watersheds. Because the agencies' mapping data are not compatible, however, staff said that the landscape assessment process was difficult. The agencies had to develop ways to merge the data, which was time-consuming and expensive. For areas outside of these watersheds, data generated by agency research are held within the sponsoring agency, so other partners sometimes do not have access to this information. For example, BLM fuel treatments are mapped in its GIS database, which the Forest Service does not have access to, and vice versa. The group noted that it would like to make all of the GIS maps available on its Web site, but according to group members, this effort is extremely resource intensive and therefore not feasible for the group to accomplish at this time with its current resources. According to the participants, BLM and the Forest Service have hired an outside consultant to serve as a repository for the GIS data.

Leverage Available Resources

The group has been successful in leveraging funds and has received over $3 million from a variety of grants. Two grants that were instrumental in getting the Uncompahgre Plateau Project started included $500,000 from

CDOW for mule deer conservation efforts and $620,000 given to the Public Lands Partnership from the Ford Foundation for community forestry. The finances of the group are handled by Uncompahgre/Com, Inc., which administers contracts, solicits bids, and pays invoices for the Uncompahgre Plateau Project and provides the partners a mechanism to pool their funds.

The Forest Service, BLM, CDOW, and the utilities support the Uncompahgre Plateau Project through various means. BLM has an assistance agreement with the group under which it can provide money to the group for activities outlined in statements of work. BLM has also given the group program funding. BLM officials noted that by having nonfederal partners, the group has a relatively easy time coming up with the nonfederal matching funds that are required with particular federal grants. In addition, BLM and the Forest Service have provided money for the native plant program. The Forest Service has used various agreements including appropriated funds spent with Wyden Amendment authority—which allows federal money to be spent on nonfederal lands—to support the efforts of the Uncompahgre Plateau Project, such as completing invasive species work across jurisdictional boundaries. The Western Area Power Administration; Tri-State Generation and Transmission Association, Inc.; and CDOW have provided money to support vegetation management projects.

The group noted that while it has had success leveraging funds in the past, it has run into difficulty acquiring funding now that the project is more mature. In addition, most grant money is for projects on the ground, so the group faces a challenge in funding its overhead costs. The Uncompahgre Plateau Project applied for a National Forest Foundation mid-capacity grant, which provides operating funding for organizations that have been working together for some time, but was unsuccessful in receiving this grant.

Provide Incentives

The Uncompahgre Plateau Project assisted a local county in establishing a cost-share program to provide incentives for private landowners to treat invasive species. Furthermore, with assistance from Colorado State University, the group has established a program to assist local growers in cultivating native plants and purchase seed from them.

Monitor Results for Accountability

According to group members, the Uncompahgre Plateau Project monitors its work on both a landscape level and a site level in the watershed where their efforts have been focused and produces an annual report for the Executive Committee and agency offices that describes their accomplishments. Some participants noted that monitoring efforts could be improved if there were more resources available. To monitor individual treatments on a site level, the group has set up a series of specific locations across a site that are monitored before, and 2 and 5 years after, a site is treated to assess whether the treatments are having anticipated results. For landscape-level monitoring the Uncompahgre Plateau Project uses GIS data to assess vegetation age classes across the watershed. The monitoring results are used in an adaptive management approach to revise management strategies in order to improve future treatments. One participant noted that the most difficult thing about conducting monitoring for collaborative groups, particularly landscape-level monitoring as the Uncompahgre Plateau Project has done, is integrating the data from different agencies.

Bibliography

Beierle, Thomas C. "The Quality of Stakeholder-Based Decisions." *Risk Analysis,* vol. 22, no. 4 (2002): 739–749.

Bell, Tom. "Broader System Urged for Fisheries Management." *Portland Press Herald,* October 10, 2005, final edition, sec. B.

Bengston, David N., George Xu, and David P. Fan. "Attitudes Toward Ecosystem Management in the United States, 1992-1998." *Society and Natural Resources,* vol. 14 (2001): 471–487.

Beyer, Jr., Dean E., Les Homan, and David N. Ewert. "Ecosystem Management in the Eastern Upper Peninsula of Michigan: A Case History." *Landscape and Urban Planning,* vol. 38 (1997): 199–211.

Bidwell, Ryan D., and Clare M. Ryan. "Collaborative Partnership Design: The Implications of Organizational Affiliation for Watershed Partnerships." *Society and Natural Resources*, vol. 19 (2006): 827–843.

Bingham, Lisa Blomgren, Tina Nabatchi, and Rosemary O'Leary. "The New Governance: Practices and Processes for Stakeholder and Citizen Participation in the Work of Government." *Public Administration Review,* vol. 65, no. 5 (2005): 547–558.

Bissix, Glyn and Judith A. Rees. "Can Strategic Ecosystem Management Succeed in Multiagency Environments?" *Ecological Applications,* vol. 11, no. 2 (2001): 570–583.

Boxer-Macomber, Lauri Diana. Too Much Sun? Emerging Challenges Presented by California and Federal Open Meeting Legislation to Public Policy Consensus-Building Processes. Sacramento, Calif.: Center for Collaborative Policy, 2003. See esp. chap. 6, "Findings."

Brick, Philip, Donald Snow, and Sarah Van de Wetering, eds. *Across the Great Divide: Explorations in Collaborative Conservation and the American West.* Washington, D.C.: Island Press, 2001.

Brody, Samuel D. "Implementing the Principles of Ecosystem Management Through Local Land Use Planning." *Population and Environment,* vol. 24, no. 6 (2003): 511.

Brody, Samuel D. "Measuring the Effects of Stakeholder Participation on the Quality of Local Plans Based on the Principles of Collaborative Ecosystem Management." *Journal of Planning Education and Research,* vol. 22 (2003): 407–419.

Brody, Samuel D., Sean B. Cash, Jennifer Dyke, and Sara Thornton. "Motivations for the Forestry Industry to Participate in Collaborative Ecosystem Management Initiatives." *Forest Policy and Economics,* vol. 8 (2006): 123–134.

Brunner, Ronald D., and Tim W. Clark. "A Practice-Based Approach to Ecosystem Management." *Conservation Biology,* vol. 11, no. 1 (1997): 48–58.

Brunner, Ronald D., Christine H. Colburn, Christina M. Cromley, Roberta A. Klein, and Elizabeth A. Olson. *Finding Common Ground: Governance and Natural Resources in the American West.* New Haven, Conn.: Yale University Press, 2002.

Brunner, Ronald D., Toddi A. Steelman, Lindy Coe-Juell, Christina M. Cromley, Christine M. Edwards, and Donna W. Tucker. *Adaptive Governance: Integrating Science, Policy, and Decision Making.* New York: Columbia University Press, 2005.

Bryan, Todd A. "Tragedy Averted: The Promise of Collaboration." *Society and Natural Resources,* vol. 17 (2004): 881–896.

Burns, Sam. "A Civic Conversation About Public Lands: Developing Community Governance." *Journal of Sustainable Forestry,* vol. 13, no. 1-2 (2001): 271–290.

Center for Collaborative Policy. "Conditions Needed to Sustain a Collaborative Policy Process." http://www.csus.edu/ccp/collaborative/sustain.htm (last accessed Jan. 23, 2008).

Cheng, Antony S., and Steven E. Daniels. "Examining the Interaction Between Geographic Scale and Ways of Knowing in Ecosystem Management: A Case Study of Place-Based Collaborative Planning." *Forest Science,* vol. 49, no. 6 (2003): 841–854.

Cheng, Antony S., and Katherine M. Mattor. "Why Won't They Come? Stakeholder Perspectives on Collaborative National Forest Planning by Participation Level." *Environmental Management,* vol. 38 (2006): 545–561.

Clagett, Matthew Patrick. "Environmental ADR and Negotiated Rule and Policy Making: Criticisms of the Institute for Environmental Conflict

Resolution and the Environmental Protection Agency." *Tulane Environmental Law Journal,* vol. 15 (2002): 409–424.

Coggins, George Cameron. "'Devolution' in Federal Land Law: Abdication by Any Other Name..." *Hastings West-Northwest Journal of Environmental Law and Policy,* vol. 3 (1996): 211–218.

Coggins, George Cameron. "Of Californicators, Quislings and Crazies: Some Perils of Devolved Collaboration." *Chronicle of Community,* vol. 2, no. 2 (1998): 27–33.

Coggins, George Cameron. "Regulating Federal Natural Resources: A Summary Case Against Devolved Collaboration." *Ecology Law Quarterly,* vol. 25 (1999): 602–610.

Comer, Robert D. "Cooperative Conservation: The Federalism Underpinnings to Public Involvement in the Management of Public Lands." *University of Colorado Law Review*, vol. 75 (2004): 1133–1157.

Congressional Research Service. *Ecosystem Management: Federal Agency Activities.* Washington, D.C.: April 19, 1994.

Conley, Alexander, and Margaret A. Moote. "Evaluating Collaborative Natural Resource Management." *Society and Natural Resources,* vol. 16 (2003): 371–386.

Cortner, Hanna J., Sam Burns, Lance R. Clark, Wendy Hinrichs Sanders, Gus Townes, and Martha Twarkins. "Governance and Institutions: Opportunities and Challenges." *Journal of Sustainable Forestry,* vol. 12, no. 3/4 (2001): 65–96.

Cortner, Hanna J., John C. Gordon, Paul G. Risser, Dennis E. Teeguarden, and Jack Ward Thomas. "Ecosystem Management: Evolving Model for Stewardship of the Nation's Natural Resources." In *Ecological Stewardship: A Common Reference for Ecosystem Management,* vol. 2, ed. R. C. Szaro, N. C. Johnson, W. T. Sexton, and A. J. Malk, 3–19. United Kingdom: Elsevier Science, Ltd., 1999.

Cortner, Hanna J. and Margaret A. Moote. *The Politics of Ecosystem Management.* Washington, D.C.: Island Press, 1999.

Coughlin, Chrissy, Merrick Hoben, Dirk Manskopf, and Shannon Quesada. "A Systematic Assessment of Collaborative Resource Management Partnerships." Master's thesis, University of Michigan, 1999.

Duane, Timothy P. "Practical Legal Issues in Community Initiated Ecosystem Management of Public Land: Community Participation in Ecosystem Management." *Ecology Law Quarterly,* vol. 24 (1997): 771–797.

Dukes, Frank. "Key Principles for Effective Collaborative Processes." Institute for Environmental Negotiation, University of Virginia, December 21, 2006.

Dukes, Frank. "Public Conflict Resolution: A Transformative Approach." *Negotiation Journal*, January 1993: 45–57.

Dukes, Frank. "What We Know About Environmental Conflict Resolution: An Analysis Based on Research." *Conflict Resolution Quarterly,* vol. 22, no. 1-2 (2004): 191–220.

Emerson, Kirk, Rosemary O'Leary, and Lisa B. Bingham. "Commentary: Comment on Frank Dukes's 'What We Know About Environmental Conflict Resolution.'" *Conflict Resolution Quarterly,* vol. 22, no. 1-2 (2004): 221–231.

Fall, Andrew, Dave Daust, and Don G. Morgan. "A Framework and Software Tool to Support Collaborative Landscape Analysis: Fitting Square Pegs into Square Holes." *Transactions in GIS,* vol. 5, no. 1 (2001): 67–86.

Frame, Tanis M., Thomas Gunton, and J. C. Day. "The Role of Collaboration in Environmental Management: An Evaluation of Land and Resource Planning in British Columbia." *Journal of Environmental Planning and Management,* vol. 47, no. 1 (2004): 59–82.

Freeman, Jody. "Collaborative Governance in the Administrative State." *UCLA Law Review,* vol. 45 (1997): 3–98.

Freeman, Richard. "The EcoFactory: The United States Forest Service and the Political Construction of Ecosystem Management." *Environmental History,* vol. 7, no. 4 (2002): 632–659.

GAO. Results Oriented Government: Practices That Can Help Enhance and Sustain Collaboration among Federal Agencies. GAO-06-15. Washington, D.C.: October 21, 2005.

Gray, Barbara. *Collaborating: Finding Common Ground for Multiparty Problems*. San Francisco: Jossey-Bass Publishers, 1989.

Gray, Gerald J., Larry Fisher, and Lynn Jungwirth. "An Introduction to Community-Based Ecosystem Management." *Journal of Sustainable Forestry,* vol. 12, no. 3/4 (2001): 25–34.

Gutrich, John, Deanna Donovan, Melissa Finucane, Will Focht, Fred Hitzhusen, Supachit Manopimoke, David McCauley, et al. "Science in the Public Process of Ecosystem Management: Lessons from Hawaii, Southeast Asia, Africa and the US Mainland." *Journal of Environmental Management,* vol. 76 (2005): 197–209.

Heikkila, Tanya, and Andrea K. Gerlak. "The Formation of Large-scale Collaborative Resource Management Institutions: Clarifying the Roles of Stakeholders, Science and Institutions." *The Policy Studies Journal,* vol. 33, no. 4 (2005): 583–611.

Helly, J. J., N. M. Kelly, D. Sutton, and T. Todd Elvins. "Collaborative Management of Natural Resources in San Diego Bay." *Coastal Management,* vol. 29, no. 2 (2001): 117–132.

Holsman, Robert H. and R. Ben Peyton. "Stakeholder Attitudes Toward Ecosystem Management in Southern Michigan." *Wildlife Society Bulletin,* vol. 31, no. 2 (2003): 349–361.

Houck, Oliver A. "On the Law of Biodiversity and Ecosystem Management." *Minnesota Law Review,* vol. 81, April (1997): 869–979.

Hummel, Mark and Bruce Freet. "Collaborative Processes for Improving Land Stewardship and Sustainability." In *Ecological Stewardship: A Common Reference for Ecosystem Management,* vol. 3, ed. W. T. Sexton, A. J. Malk, R. C. Szaro, and N. C. Johnson, 97–129. United Kingdom: Elsevier Science, Ltd., 1999.

Imperial, Mark T. "Analyzing Institutional Arrangements for Ecosystem-Based Management: Lessons from the Rhode Island Salt Ponds SAM Plan." *Coastal Management,* vol. 27, no. 1 (1999): 31–56.

Innes, Judith E. "Consensus Building: Clarifications for the Critics." *Planning Theory,* vol. 3, no. 1 (2004): 5–20.

Jackson, Laurie Skuba. "Contemporary Public Involvement: Toward a Strategic Approach." *Local Environment,* vol. 6, no. 2 (2001): 135–147.

Johnson, Kathleen M., Al Abee, Gerry Alcock, David Behler, Brien Culhane, Ken Holtje, Don Howlett, George Martinez, and Kathleen Picarelli. "Management Perspectives on Regional Cooperation." In *Ecological Stewardship: A Common Reference for Ecosystem Management,* vol. 3, ed. W. T. Sexton, A. J. Malk, R. C. Szaro, and N. C. Johnson, 155–180. United Kingdom: Elsevier Science, Ltd., 1999.

Johnson, Nels. "Legal Perspectives." In *Ecological Stewardship: A Common Reference for Ecosystem Management,* vol. 1, ed. N. C. Johnson, A. J. Malk, R. C. Szaro, and W. T. Sexton, 107–113. United Kingdom: Elsevier Science, Ltd., 1999.

Kagan, Robert A. "Political and Legal Obstacles to Collaborative Ecosystem Planning." *Ecology Law Quarterly,* vol. 24 (1997): 871–875.

Keiter, Robert B. "NEPA and the Emerging Concept of Ecosystem Management on the Public Lands." *Land and Water Law Review,* vol. 25, no. 1 (1990): 43–60.

Keiter, Robert B., Ted Boling, and Louise Milkman. "Legal Perspectives on Ecosystem Management: Legitimizing a New Federal Land Management Policy." In *Ecological Stewardship: A Common Reference for Ecosystem Management,* vol. 3, ed. W. T. Sexton, A. J. Malk, R. C. Szaro, and N. C. Johnson, 9–41. United Kingdom: Elsevier Science, Ltd., 1999.

Keough, Heather L. and Dale J. Blahna. “Achieving Integrative, Collaborative Ecosystem Management.” *Conservation Biology,* vol. 20, no. 5 (2006): 1373–1382.

Keystone Center. “The Keystone National Policy Dialogue on Ecosystem Management: Final Report.” The Keystone Center, Colorado, October 1996.

Knight, Richard L. and Peter B. Landres, eds. *Stewardship Across Boundaries.* Washington, D.C.: Island Press, 1998.

Koontz, Tomas M., Toddi A. Steelman, JoAnn Carmin, Katrina Smith Korfmacher, Cassandra Moseley, and Craig W. Thomas. *Collaborative Environmental Management: What Roles for Government?* Washington, D.C.: Resources for the Future, 2004.

Koontz, Tomas M., and Craig W. Thomas. “What Do We Know and Need to Know about the Environmental Outcomes of Collaborative Management?” Public Administration Review, December 2006: 111–121.

Korfmacher, Katrina Smith. “What’s the Point of Partnering?” *The American Behavioral Scientist,* vol. 44, no. 4 (2000): 548–566.

Lachapelle, Paul R., Stephen F. McCool, and Michael E. Patterson. “Barriers to Effective Natural Resource Planning in a ‘Messy’ World.” *Society and Natural Resources,* vol. 16 (2003): 473–490.

Lawless, W. F., M. Bergman, and N. Feltovich. “Consensus Seeking Versus Truth Seeking.” *Practice Periodical of Hazardous, Toxic, and Radioactive Waste Management,* vol. 9, no. 1 (2005): 59–70.

Leach, William D. “Building a Theory of Collaboration.” In *Effective Collaboration for Environmental Change: Making Sense of an Emerging Socio-Ecological Movement,* Community-Based Collaboratives Research Consortium, forthcoming.

Leach, William D. “Collaborative Public Management and Democracy: Evidence from Western Watershed Partnerships.” *Public Administration Review,* December 2006: 100–110.

Leach, William D. “Public Involvement in UDSA Forest Service Policymaking: A Literature Review.” *Journal of Forestry,* January/February 2006, 43–49.

Leach, William D. “Surveying Diverse Stakeholder Groups.” *Society and Natural Resources,* vol. 15 (2002): 641–649.

Leach, William D. "Theories about Consensus-Based Conservation." *Conservation Biology,* vol. 20, no. 2 (2006): 573–575.

Leach, William D., and Neil W. Pelkey. "Making Watershed Partnerships Work: A Review of the Empirical Literature." *Journal of Water Resources Planning and Management,* vol. 127, no. 6 (2001): 378–385.

Leach, William D., Neil W. Pelkey, and Paul A. Sabatier. "Stakeholder Partnerships as Collaborative Policymaking: Evaluation Criteria Applied to Watershed Management in California and Washington." *Journal of Policy Analysis and Management,* vol. 21, no. 4 (2002): 645–670.

Leshy, John. "Public Lands." American Law Institute—American Bar Association Continuing Legal Education Course of Study, February 13–15, 2002.

Linden, Russell M. *Working Across Boundaries: Making Collaboration Work in Government and Nonprofit Organizations.* San Francisco, Calif.: Jossey-Bass, 2002.

Lubell, Mark. "Collaborative Watershed Management: A View from the Grassroots." *Policy Studies Journal,* vol. 32, no. 3 (2004): 341–361.

Lugenbill, Chris Herman. "An Interorganizational Management Strategy for Collaborative Stewardship." Ph.D. diss., Colorado Technical University, 2003.

Lysak, Tetyana, and Edward P. Weber. "Collaboratives, Wicked Problems, and Institutional Design: Different Theories, Same Lessons." Washington State University, submitted for publication, December 29, 2006.

MacEachren, Alan M. "Cartography and GIS: Facilitating Collaboration." *Progress in Human Geography,* vol. 24, no. 3 (2000): 445–456.

MacCleery, Douglas W., and Dennis C. Le Master. "The Historical Foundation and Evolving Context for Natural Resource Management on Federal Lands." In *Ecological Stewardship: A Common Reference for Ecosystem Management,* vol. 2, ed. R. C. Szaro, N. C. Johnson, W. T. Sexton, and A. J. Malk, 517–556. United Kindgom: Elsevier Science, Ltd., 1999.

Malk, Andrew. "Processes for Collaboration." In *Ecological Stewardship: A Common Reference for Ecosystem Management,* vol. 1, ed. N. C. Johnson, A. J. Malk, R. C. Szaro, and W. T. Sexton, 129–134. United Kingdom: Elsevier Science, Ltd., 1999.

Malone, Charles R. "Ecosystem Management Policies in State Government of the USA." *Landscape and Urban Planning,* vol. 48 (2000): 57–64.

Manring, Nancy J. "Collaborative Resource Management: Organizational Benefits and Individual Costs." *Administration and Society,* vol. 30, no. 3 (1998): 2742–90.

Margerum, Richard D., and Debra Whitall. "The Challenges and Implications of Collaborative Management on a River Basin Scale." *Journal of Environmental Planning and Management,* vol. 47, no. 3 (2004): 4074–27.

McClosky, Michael. "Local Communities and the Management of Public Forests." *Ecology Law Quarterly,* vol. 25 (1999): 624–629.

McKinney, Matthew, Craig Fitch, and Will Harmon. "Regionalism in the West: An Inventory and Assessment." *Public Land and Resources Law Review,* vol. 23 (2002): 101–123.

Meffe, Gary K. "Biological and Ecological Dimensions: Overview." In Ecological Stewardship: A Common Reference for Ecosystem *Management,* vol. 1, ed. N. C. Johnson, A. J. Malk, R. C. Szaro, and W. T. Sexton, 39–44. United Kingdom: Elsevier Science, Ltd., 1999.

Mog, Justin Matthew. "Managing Development Programs for Sustainability: Integrating Development and Research Through Adaptive Management." Society and Natural Resources, vol. 19 (2006): 531–546.

Moody, James Bradfield, and Mark Dodgson. "Managing Complex Collaborative Projects: Lessons from the Development of a New Satellite." Journal of Technology Transfer, vol. 31 (2006): 567–588.

Moore, Elizabeth A., and Tomas M. Koontz. "A Typology of Collaborative Watershed Groups: Citizen-Based, Agency-Based, and Mixed Partnerships." Society and Natural Resources, vol. 16 (2003): 451-460.

Mortenson, Kristin G., and Richard S. Krannich. "Wildlife Managers and Public Involvement: Letting the Crazy Aunt Out." *Human Dimensions of Wildlife,* vol. 6 (2001): 277–290.

O'Neill, Karen M. "Can Watershed Management Unite Town and Country?" Society and Natural Resources, vol. 18 (2005): 241–253.

Office of Management and Budget and Council on Environmental Quality. Memorandum on Environmental Conflict Resolution. Washington, D.C., November 28, 2005.

Paulson, Deborah D. "Collaborative Management of Public Rangeland in Wyoming: Lessons in Co-Management." *Professional Geographer,* vol. 50, no. 3 (1998): 301–315.

Payton, Michelle A., David C. Fulton, and Dorothy H. Anderson. "Influence of Place Attachment and Trust on Civic Action: A Study at Sherburne National Wildlife Refuge." *Society and Natural Resources,* vol. 18 (2005): 511–528.

Peterson, M. Nils, Markus J. Peterson, and Tarla Rai Peterson. "Conservation and the Myth of Consensus." *Conservation Biology,* vol. 19, no. 3 (2005): 762–767.

Plummer, Ryan. "Sharing the Management of a River Corridor: A Case Study of the Comanagement Process." *Society and Natural Resources,* vol. 19 (2006): 709–712.

Raedeke, Andrew H., J. Sanford Rikoon, and Charles H. Nilon. "Ecosystem Management and Landowner Concern About Regulations: A Case Study in the Missouri Ozarks." *Society and Natural Resources,* vol. 14 (2001): 741–759.

Ramirez, Ricardo and Maria Fernandez. "Facilitation of Collaborative Resource Management: Reflections from Practice." *Systemic Practice and Action Research,* vol. 18, no. 1 (2005): 5–20.

Rigg, Catherine M. "Orchestrating Ecosystem Management: Challenges and Lessons from Sequoia National Forest." *Conservation Biology,* vol. 15, no. 1 (2001): 78–90.

Rodriguez, Daniel B. "The Role of Legal Innovation in Ecosystem Management: Perspectives from American Local Government Law." *Ecology Law Quarterly,* vol. 24 (1997): 745–769.

Ryan, Clare M. and Jacqueline S. Klug. "Collaborative Watershed Planning in Washington State: Implementing the Watershed Planning Act." *Journal of Environmental Planning and Management,* vol. 48, no. 4 (2005): 491–506.

Sayre, Nathan F. "Interacting Effects of Landownership, Land Use, and Endangered Species on Conservation of Southwestern U.S. Rangelands." *Conservation Biology,* vol. 19, no. 3 (2005): 783–792.

Scarlett, P. Lynn. "A New Approach to Conservation: The Case for the Four Cs." *Natural Resources and Environment,* vol. 17, no. 1 (2002-2003): 73–113.

Scheutt, Michael A., Steve W. Selen, and Deborah S. Carr. "Making It Work: Keys to Successful Collaboration in Natural Resource Management." *Environmental Management,* vol. 27, no. 4 (2001): 587–593.

Schusler, Tania M., Daniel J. Decker, and Max J. Pfeffer. "Social Learning for Collaborative Natural Resource Management." *Society and Natural Resources,* vol. 15 (2003): 309–326.

Selin, Steve, Michael Scheutt, and Debbie Carr. "Modeling Stakeholder Perceptions of Collaborative Initiative Effectiveness." *Society and Natural Resources,* vol. 13, no. 8 (2000): 735–745

Sexton, William T., Robert C. Szaro, and Nels C. Johnson. "The Ecological Stewardship Project: A Vision for Sustainable Resource Management." In Ecological Stewardship: A Common Reference for Ecosystem *Management,* vol. 1, ed. N. C. Johnson, A. J. Malk, R. C. Szaro, and W. T. Sexton, 1–8. Elsevier Science, Ltd., 1999.

Singleton, Sara. "Collaborative Environmental Planning in the American West: The Good, the Bad and the Ugly." *Environmental Politics,* vol. 11, no. 3 (2002): 54–75.

Smith, Patrick D. and Maureen H. McDonough. "Beyond Public Participation: Fairness in Natural Resource Decision Making." *Society and Natural Resources,* vol. 14 (2001): 239–249.

Smith, Patrick D., Maureen H. McDonough, and Michael T. Mang. "Ecosystem Management and Public Participation: Lessons from the Field." *Journal of Forestry,* vol. 97, no. 10 (1999): 32–39.

Smutko, L. Steven. "Environmental Dispute Resolution Processes for Resource Conservation." Department of Agricultural and Resource Economics, North Carolina State University.

Susskind, Lawrence E., and Jennifer Thomas-Larmer. "Conducting Conflict Assessment." In *The Consensus Building Handbook: A Comprehensive Guide to Reaching Agreement,* ed. Lawrence E. Susskind, Sarah McKearnan, and Jennifer Thomas-Larmer. Thousand Oaks, Calif.: Sage Publications, 1999.

Swanson, Louis E. "Rural Policy and Direct Local Participation: Democracy, Inclusiveness, Collective Agency, and Locality-Based Policy." *Rural Sociology,* vol. 66, no. 1 (2001): 1–21.

Thompson, Jan R., William F. Elmendorf, Maureen H. McDonough, and Lisa L. Burban. "Participation and Conflict: Lessons Learned from Community Forestry." *Journal of Forestry,* June 2005, 174–178.

Thompson, Jonathan R., Mark D. Anderson, and Norman Johnson. "Ecosystem Management across Ownerships: The Potential for Collision with Antitrust Laws." *Conservation Biology,* vol. 18, no. 6 (2004): 1475–1481.

Tilt, Whitney. "Collaboration in Our Backyard: Lessons from Community-Based Collaboration in the West." *The Quivira Coalition Newsletter,* vol. 7, no. 2 (2005): 22–30.

Tilt, Whitney. "Getting Federal Land Management Agencies to the Collaborative Table: Barriers and Remedies." Sonoran Institute, 2005.

Tipa, Gail and Richard Welch. "Comanagement of Natural Resources: Issues of Definition from and Indigenous Community Perspective." *Journal of Applied Behavorial Science,* vol. 42, no 3 (2006): 373–391.

Twarkins, Martha, Larry Fisher, and Tahnee Robertson. "Public Involvement in Forest Management Planning: A View from the Northeast." *Journal of Sustainable Forestry,* vol. 13, no. 1/2 (2001): 237–251.

U.S. Institute for Environmental Conflict Resolution. *Off-Highway Vehicle Use and Collaboration: Lessons Learned from Project Implementation,* edited by Larry Fisher. Tucson, Arizona, August 26, 2005.

Waage, Sissel. "Collaborative Salmon Recovery Planning: Examining Decision Making and Implementation in Northeastern Oregon." *Society and Natural Resources,* vol. 16 (2003): 295–307.

Walker, Peter A. and Patrick Hurley. "Collaboration Derailed: The Politics of 'Community-Based' Resource Management in Nevada County." *Society and Natural Resources,* vol. 17 (2004): 735–751.

Weber, Edward P. Bringing Society Back In: Grassroots Ecosystem Management, Accountability, and Sustainable Communities. Cambridge, Mass.: The MIT Press, 2003.

Weber, Edward P. "The Question of Accountability in Historical Perspective: From Jackson to Contemporary Grassroots Ecosystem Management." *Administration and Society,* vol. 31, no. 4 (1999): 451–495.

Weber, Edward P. "A Theory of Institutional Change for Tough Cases of Collaboration: 'Ideas' in the Blackfoot Watershed." Washington State University, submitted for publication, December 20, 2006.

Weber, Edward P. "Wicked Problems, Knowledge Challenges, and Collaborative Capacity Builders in Network Settings." *Public Administration Review* (forthcoming).

Weber, Edward P., Nicholas P. Lovrich, and Michael Gaffney. "Assessing Collaborative Capacity in a Multidimensional World." *Administration and Society,* vol. 39, no. 2 (2007): 194–220.

Weber, Edward P., Nicholas P. Lovrich, and Michael Gaffney. "Collaboration, Enforcement, and Endangered Species: A Framework for Assessing Collaborative Problem-Solving Capacity." *Society and Natural Resources,* vol. 18 (2005): 677–698.

Webler, Thomas, Seth Tuler, Ingrid Shockey, Paul Stern, and Robert Beattie. "Participation by Local Governmental Officials in Watershed Management Planning." *Society and Natural Resources,* vol. 16 (2003): 105–121.

Western Governors' Association. "Collaborative Conservation Strategies: Legislative Case Studies from Across the West." Western Governors' Association White Paper, June 2006.

Wilson, Randall K. "Collaboration in Context: Rural Change and Community Forestry in the Four Corners." *Society and Natural Resources,* vol. 19 (2006): 53–70.

Wondolleck, Julia M. and Steven L. Yaffee. *Making Collaboration Work: Lessons from Innovation in Natural Resource Management.* Washington, D.C.: Island Press, 2000.

Yaffee, Steven L. "Regional Cooperation: A Strategy for Achieving Ecological Stewardship." In *Ecological Stewardship: A Common Reference for Ecosystem Management,* vol. 3, ed. W. T. Sexton, A. J. Malk, R. C. Szaro, and N. C. Johnson, 31–153. United Kingdom: Elsevier Science, Ltd., 1999.

Yaffee, Steven L. "Three Faces of Ecosystem Management." *Conservation Biology,* vol. 13, no. 4 (1999): 713–725.

References

[1] The Forest Service initially received stewardship contracting authority first as a pilot program in 1998, while BLM received it in 2003. For a description of agency use of stewardship contracting authority, see GAO, *Federal Land Management: Additional Guidance on Community Involvement Could Enhance Effectiveness of Stewardship Contracting*, GAO-04-652 (Washington, D.C.: June 14, 2004).

[2] The Forest Service also uses collaboration in forest planning. This involves people working together to share knowledge and resources to describe and achieve desired conditions for National Forest System lands and for associated social, ecological, and economic systems in a plan area.

[3] The Federal Grants and Cooperative Agreement Act directs federal agencies to use grants when the principal purpose of the relationship is to transfer value to a nonfederal recipient to carry out a public purpose rather than to acquire property or services for the benefit of the federal government. Agencies are to use cooperative agreements when the agency will be substantially involved in carrying out the agreement, and grants if such involvement is not expected.

[4] The agencies are required to consult with the National Marine Fisheries Service for actions that may affect threatened and endangered species under the service's jurisdiction. These include marine mammals, marine turtles, marine and anadromous fish, and marine invertebrates and plants.

[5] The term "take" means to harass, harm, pursue, hunt, shoot, wound, kill, trap, capture, or collect, or to attempt to engage in any such conduct. Regulations implementing the act define "harm" to mean an act which actually kills or injures wildlife. Such acts may include significant habitat modification or degradation where it actually kills or injures wildlife by impairing essential behavior patterns.

[6] The total number of conservation-related programs can be defined in several ways. The Congressional Research Service describes some programs as having subprograms, while others were created by administrative action. In addition to the 20 programs, Congress has authorized other discretionary programs that often have a specific geographic focus.

[7] These sources include our report: GAO, Results-Oriented Government: Practices That Can Help Enhance and Sustain Collaboration among Federal Agencies, GAO-06-15 (Washington, D.C.: Oct. 21, 2005).

[8] The five objectives are: (1) maintain and enhance cooperative and innovative management projects, programs, and agreements between tribal, public, and private interests in the CMPA; (2) promote grazing, recreation, historic, and other uses that are sustainable; (3) conserve, protect, and ensure traditional access to cultural, gathering, religious, and archaeological sites by the Burns Paiute Tribe on federal lands and to promote cooperation with private landowners; (4) ensure the conservation, protection, and improved management of the ecological, social, and economic environment of the CMPA, including geological, biological, wildlife, riparian, and scenic resources; and (5) promote and foster cooperation, communication, and understanding and to reduce conflict between Steens Mountain users and interests.

[9] This is part of the Kennedy School of Government at Harvard University.

[10] The Ford Foundation grant was to the Public Lands Partnership, which funded the Uncompahgre Plateau Project from that amount.

[11] Congress enacted the Federal Advisory Committee Act in 1972 in response to two principal concerns: (1) federal advisory committees were proliferating without adequate review, oversight, or accountability and (2) certain special interests had too much influence over federal agency decision makers. The act generally applies to committees established or used by federal agencies for the purpose of obtaining advice or recommendations.

[12] S. 232, a bill pending in the Senate, would extend this authority permanently for the Forest Service.

[13] John R. Ehrmann and Juliana E. Birkhoff, *Supplemental Analysis of Day Two Facilitated Discussion Sessions*, White House Conference on Cooperative Conservation (Dec. 28, 2005).

[14] The policy group provides overall policy direction to an executive-level task force that manages the initiative.

[15] BLM recently determined that it would review this series, as it is almost 10 years old. According to Interior and BLM officials, the agency is determining the most effective way to deliver the training.

[16] An interagency task force, convened by the U.S. Institute for Environmental Conflict Resolution at the request of CEQ in 2003, developed the principles included in the guidance. The task force effort paralleled the development of the Cooperative Conservation initiative.
[17] For the Web site, see http://cooperativeconservation.gov.
[18] Council on Environmental Quality, *Collaboration in NEPA: A Handbook for NEPA Practitioners* (Washington, D.C.: October 2007). According to Forest Service officials, the agency is in the process of putting its NEPA policy into federal regulations, which will emphasize collaboration in alternative development as well as other aspects of the NEPA process.
[19] National Environmental Conflict Resolution Advisory Committee, Final Report Submitted to the U.S. Institute for Environmental Conflict Resolution of the Morris K. Udall Foundation (Tucson, Ariz.: April 2005).
[20] For example, the Federal Grants and Cooperative Agreements Act provides, in pertinent part, that an executive agency must use a procurement contract when: (1) the principal purpose of the instrument is to acquire (by purchase, lease, or barter) property or services for the direct benefit or use of the U. S. government; or (2) the agency decides in a specific instance that the use of a procurement contract is appropriate.

Appendix I

[21] GAO, Results-Oriented Government: Practices That Can Help Enhance and Sustain Collaboration among Federal Agencies, GAO-06-15 (Washington, D.C.: Oct. 21, 2005).

Appendix II

[22] The Blackfoot Challenge was established in 1991 and formally chartered in 1993.
[23] The average flow of the river is 1,968 cubic feet per second; in 2000, a drought year, the average flow was 1,261 cubic feet per second.
[24] In Montana, riparian lands, or lands located along a river corridor, are frequently privately owned, while the streambed is often owned by the state.

[25] The 11 states include California, Colorado, Idaho, Montana, Nevada, North Dakota, Oregon, South Dakota, Utah, Washington, and Wyoming.

[26] In *County of San Miguel v. MacDonald*, the county and several environmental and public interest groups have challenged the U.S. Fish and Wildlife Service's determination that listing of the Gunnison sage grouse under the Endangered Species Act was not warranted. In *Center for Biological Diversity v. U.S. Fish and Wildlife Service*, an environmental group is challenging the agency's rejection of a petition to list the Mono Basin area sage grouse as endangered or threatened. In *Western Watersheds Project v. U.S. Fish and Wildlife Service*, several environmental groups challenged the agency's decision not to list the greater sage grouse under the Endangered Species Act. In December 2007, the court held that the agency's decision was unauthorized because it had not been based on the best available science, as the Endangered Species Act requires. The court directed the agency to reconsider the petitions.

[27] Money from the Sand County Foundation came through the Bradley Fund for the Environment, a partnership between Sand County Foundation and the Lynde and Harry Bradley Foundation.

[28] Congress enacted Federal Advisory Committee Act in 1972 in response to two principal concerns: (1) that federal advisory committees were proliferating without adequate review, oversight, or accountability and (2) that certain special interests had too much influence over federal agency decision makers. The act generally applies to committees established or utilized by federal agencies for the purpose of obtaining advice or recommendations.

[29] The project will also test national fire data for the LANDFIRE project, which is a database and related models being developed by the Forest Service and BLM to gather consistent national data on vegetation conditions and related fuel conditions.

[30] Pub. L. No. 106-399, Title I, § 101, 114 Stat. 1658 (2000).

[31] The Steens Act also designates three new Wild and Scenic Rivers, adds new segments to existing Wild and Scenic Rivers, creates a Redband Trout Reserve, and designates 900,000 acres of federal land off-limits to mineral and geothermal extraction.

[32] Specifically, the act "authorized to be appropriated $25,000,000 from the land and water conservation fund established under section 2 of the Land and Water Conservation Fund Act of 1965 … to provide funds for the acquisition of land and interests in land … and to enter into non-development easements and conservation easements" as provided elsewhere under the act.

[33] Conservation incentive payments under the Steens Act may include technical assistance, cost-share payments, incentive payments, and education.

INDEX

C

F

G

H

I

N

O

P

Q

R

S